LIVING HOPE

A story of unwavering faith when life
unexpectedly changes

ERIC FOUST

ISBN: 979-8-9910939-0-3

Book Design: Sandy Adler

Book Formatting: Beth Chiles

To Erika, Joel, and Seth, you have been my strength on this unexpected journey. Mom loved you deeply.

Contents

Foreword   vii
Introduction   xi

PART I
Mercy   1

PART II
Granite Bay   59

PART III
Enloe Rehabilitation   97

PART IV
Home   119

PART V
Fully Home   145

PART VI
After Death   159

About the Author   167

Foreword

Of all the people the Lord could have led me to in those first days at a new college, at such a pivotal time of total life transformation and change, I still feel awe and gratitude that Judy Foust (then Burling) was one of the first and most important.

She was petite and pretty, with perfectly feathered, strawberry blonde hair, and eyes that actually did sparkle as she took in the measure of me from our first encounter. Her face was so vital and intelligent, and she was keenly interested in helping me through the frustrations and challenges of being an overwhelmed new college student who didn't know a single person at that point. But what she was really, keenly interested in, then and always, was ME... she had this intuitive gift for looking through me, reading my feelings, and then she was all invested in helping me solve problems and process through them, even if it took us into the wee hours on a school night.

She was a passionate, relatively new Christian, so her love for Jesus was fresh and beautiful. We were both in a place of awe and wonder at the forgiveness and mercy of the Lord, and our hearts connected so deeply around our faith, around the joy of salvation, around the Bible, and also around how blessed we were to be at Crown (then St. Paul Bible) College, where we could grow and study and learn in such a safe, sweet environment of like-minded young believers.

Of course, since then I learned I wasn't the only person Judy was keenly interested in. I realized that's how Judy saw EVERYONE, even strangers, and that this was indeed her special gift, to really SEE people and to dig in and understand their core struggles, and then process through until there was resolution and resolve. It was her unique ability and the way she influenced others, and brought her love for Jesus into every life she could possibly touch. She was invariably kind, and had a tenacious loyalty that made her hold on long and hard to the people she cared about.

It was during our college days that Judy began getting to know this guy, Eric, and we would process their relationship and her feelings and thoughts for hours on end. Of course, things DID work out, and Eric and Judy married and became two of our closest and dearest lifelong friends. The four of us shared new marriage adventures together, and our first-born daughters came into the world a week apart, so we shared intimately the challenges and joys of parenting. We were all devoted followers of Christ in full-time ministry as well, so our connection was deep, encouraging, and life-giving.

I share this because I want everyone who picks up and reads this astonishing book Eric has written to have that backdrop of these two wonderful people to set behind the story. Eric sent me the following chapters a bit at a time, so I was left hanging as I waited for him to write the next section so I could continue the story! Even though I lived much of this history with them, I found myself pulled right in by the engaging, narrative style, and I raced through as if I didn't already know what would happen. His words take you right inside their love story, back in time to their first encounters with each other, through growing love and romance, marriage and family and great trials and tests of faith and love. As a pastor and teacher, Eric weaves in his own personal revelations and experiences, along with profound truth and insight into the goodness and presence of God that is the crux of the entire story, with great wisdom and clarity. I laughed and cried HARD, and was deeply moved and inspired by Eric's raw, honest, vulnerable depiction of their journey through so much joy and sorrow. Many of the details were new to me that so vividly describe the months and days leading up to the end, and I felt both deeply grateful and also cut to the heart as Eric's words brought me into their private, painful experiences after Judy's stroke.

This is a story of married love when Christ is at the center. It's a story of two very imperfect people who hang on and grow closer, deeper and stronger through unbearable trials because of their mutual submission to something so much greater than themselves. It's a story of the overwhelming uncertainty of life, which can be struck by temptation and tragedy in a heartbeat, but which can also be overcome by the power, grace and love of Jesus, Who remains faithful and unchanging both now and forever. It is a skillfully written tribute that demonstrates to the rest of us how to live out our faith in the darkest of days. I pray this beautiful story brings hope and strength to many with that very message, especially those facing their own season of pain and loss.

With so much respect and love,
Sandy Adler

Introduction

While we have the thought lodged in the recesses of our mind that life, as we know it, can be altered and radically changed in the blink of an eye, we seldom live as if that's an actual possibility. Instead, we live the hours and days of our lives as if everything will continue as is, according to plan with nothing hindering the uninterrupted momentum of the current day from being carried forward into the next. We schedule, prepare, and calendarize our days with a mindful sense of responsible regularity and understandably so. It would seem slightly irrational to do otherwise. The thought of purposefully or strategically creating space for catastrophe, chaos, or the unthinkable to disrupt the flow of our days feels completely unhealthy and abnormal. We certainly don't plan for tragedy and trauma. Disruptions, diagnoses, detours, and departures from the norm seem insignificantly distant from us...until they happen. Then, everything that was stops. The life we were so expectantly living unexpectedly changes.

What so abruptly flips the script of our lives is how unprepared we are for the unexpected. When the phone call comes, when the diagnosis is delivered, when trauma invades, when that text illuminates our screen with heart wrenching news and time simultaneously ceases and steals our next breath in the same instance, we are taken aback in shock while our nervous system seems completely uncertain of the correct emotional response. We are unwelcomingly thrust into a new world of pain, loss, grief, and confusion. Anger, sadness, disbelief, disappointment, denial and tears, gut wrenching tears, all vie for the dominate emotional reaction to be expressed but all end up intertwined together. Pouring out however and whenever they can, regardless of the moment or the "appropriate" timing.

As I put my thoughts and our story to paper, I do so with the resounding awareness that many have lived a similar story but through their own unique perspective and life lens. Still others have encountered life altering events that are far worse and with much more traumatic outcomes. Yet all of us, no matter the degree or depth of life's unimaginable interruptions, are forced to face the question of what now? Where do we go from here? What's next? How do we go on? We step precariously from one moment to the next wondering if we'll ever experience the presence of happiness or the reality of joy again? Will we find ourselves awake every single night at 2:00am, staring at the ceiling faintly lit by the nightlight, because darkness seems way too invasive with our minds ceaselessly contemplating every possible scenario, true or not, that we now find ourselves having to navigate? Has this detour in our journey of life become our permanent road to travel, our new norm? I guess the truth is that not all those questions will find answers which, in many ways, makes them that much harder to face. But also, I believe, that it's in the searching, the questioning, the uncertainty, and even in the darkness of night that we can encounter hope, faith, and strength to move forward. There comes an internal urging to press in rather than give up. All the aforementioned emotions don't evaporate but they can dissipate in their control over us.

Judy has repeatedly expressed her conviction that there is a privilege to pain. There are benefits enjoyed through the struggle of pain. Now what you need to know about Judy is that she doesn't communicate that conviction haphazardly, nonchalantly or callously. She isn't denying pain's reality or advocating for the numbing of our senses when we are coping with grief and sorrow that follow loss and trauma of any kind. Nor is she voicing a form of religious suppression that seeks to pretend away the truth that painful and bad things can happen to anyone with deep hurt. Rather, there is an internal anchor in Judy that firmly holds to the belief that priceless core elements of who we are can be forged in the intense heat of heartache, grief, and loss. We discover what makes life have value, separating it from the insignificant. We are able to redefine the purpose of our days through different constructs than previously experienced. Through the scars, seen and unseen, there can emerge a heartfelt story that personifies limitless love, healing hope, relentless resilience, and courageous contentment. Even when you're in the trial of your life.

PART I

Mercy

Thursday, September 2, 2021, is etched in Judy and I's mental calendar as the last day of normalcy. Nothing seemed noticeably out of the ordinary for Judy on that day. While she had mentioned in the afternoon of the previous day that she had experienced, as Judy described it, "some unusual purple flashes of light" in her vision, she had in all other ways felt normal. So, our Thursday routine began without a concern or care. As I went to work at a large local church in an executive leadership capacity, Judy reported to work as an Administrative Assistant/Front Desk receptionist for a local hearing aids business.

For Judy, being a Front Desk receptionist was far more than simply a work role that she occupied for five days a week. It was who she was. Judy loves people and the more opportunity she had to engage, appreciate, value, and give attention to those who came into her midst, the more she thrived. There not a client, vendor, visitor, or guest that did not receive Judy's full smile, sweet disposition, and who wasn't made to feel like they were the most important person in the room. She was an extrovert extraordinaire. The amazing truth about Judy is that it didn't matter whether she was at work, greeting attenders at the door of our church, or connecting with the staff at a local restaurant, everybody was a friend waiting to be made. Her engaging extroverted personality combined with her quick wit and dry humor were captivating and enthralling. Judy loved her co-workers and clients and took great pride in being available and accessible in her role.

Which is why it was slightly unnerving when she came home on that Thursday for lunch complaining of a potential migraine and nausea and made the difficult decision that she would be unable to return to work that afternoon. In the present age of COVID-19, it's tough to identify symptoms and feel confident in self-diagnosis. But feeling fairly certain that these weren't COVID symptoms that were running through her system, she took an afternoon nap. Hoping that by gaining some extra and helpful sleep, it would remedy her situation.

When Judy awoke from her nap a couple of hours later, she was relieved that her headache and nausea had, indeed, somewhat subsided, enough that she was able to eat a light dinner and had the energy to FaceTime our daughter, Erika, and son-in-law, Tim. All three of our children and their spouses live out of state and so anytime we connect with them it is a special gift for us. As Judy conversed, all seemed well. Her conversation was engaging and witty, insightful and inquisitive. From all indications, Judy was just fine and had overcome whatever bug, upset stomach, or weird physical unsettledness she had experienced earlier. We had no suspicion of what was to come.

At 1:00am on Friday, September 3, Judy got up to use the bathroom. Certainly nothing out of the ordinary as this was a nightly routine and had been for years. A couple of times a night Judy would make the quick jaunt to the bathroom and back. So accustomed she was to this that she could traverse the steps from bedside to bathroom and back again on the darkest of nights with stealth-like agility, often without even disturbing me from my sleep. This time however, after a few steps she lost her balance, stumbled into the dresser near the end of the bed and staggered into the bathroom. A few minutes later, Judy returned to bed. In my lack of awareness and half-asleep stupor, I asked her the ignorant question if she was alright. She calmly asserted that she was fine and probably not quite awake when she got up and simply lost her balance. She reassured me that there was nothing to worry about.

A few hours later at 4:00am, she felt the need to revisit the bathroom. Judy pulled the sheets back, swung her legs over the edge of the bed, sat up and with every intention to stand, she planted her feet on the familiar carpeting. As she stood, her legs crumpled underneath her and she fell to the floor, hitting the bedside nightstand on the way down, jarring me awake. She quickly tried to regain a semblance of composure and physical control of her body. With an unsteady posture, I noticed her take a few uncoordinated, off-balance steps in the direction of the bathroom when her legs gave out again and she fell hard onto the floor a second time. In that rapid sequence of events, time ceased. The world became irrelevant beyond her contorted body in front of me. With an immediate surge of adrenaline, I leaped from the bed and was on the floor next to her in a single bound. More impulsively than intentionally, Judy attempted to pull her legs up under her body so that she could position herself on her hands and knees. But her legs wouldn't cooperate. Rather than obeying the muscular and reflexive command to pull in and support her weight, her legs stayed sprawled on the floor, unresponsive to Judy's physical request and expectation. No matter how hard she tried, her legs would not act in partnership with her brain.

It was at this inopportune time that I, again, voiced my ignorance by asking, *"why don't your legs work?"* As if Judy were engaging in some heinous prank in the middle of the night by creating a ruse that her legs weren't working just to get a panicked reaction from me. By all standards, it was a ridiculous and insensitive question to ask if ever there was one given the severity of the moment. Looking back, I've come to terms with the fact that I wasn't asking the question from a place of logic and reason, expecting a logical and reasonable answer in response. It wasn't the place for interactive conversation. But rather, I was asking the question from having had the initial door of trauma and shock pushed open with no going back and adrenaline overpowering mental acumen. In this frozen segment of time, the need which prompted Judy to get up in the first place was now released uncontrollably. Shocked and embarrassed by this sudden unbelievable nightmare playing out in real life, Judy was sitting in soaked pajamas as urine pooled around her on the floor.

"*What's wrong with me?*" Judy asked in alarm with moderately slurred speech. Here was the first chance I had to look into her eyes and see her face. Her usually bright blue eyes, now swallowed up with dark and enlarged pupils, were clearly expressing fear. The left side of her face already showed signs of drooping. Her mouth which so easily flashed that welcoming smile was now slightly lopsided. I attempted to calmly reassure her, "*It's going to be ok. I'm going to get you to the hospital. It's going to be ok.*" But I knew that we had been thrust into turbulent waters. All symptoms indicated stroke. The foundation of our lives had begun to unravel.

Possibly from old TV commercials or, perhaps, from that one mandatory biology course I reluctantly took in college, I had a faint recollection regarding stroke signs and how to respond. I knew enough to know that time was critical. Instantly, time which had come to a stop in the chaos of our bedroom now seemed to have been catapulted into hyper speed. Everything was in motion. The clock was running. Rather than dialing 9-1-1, I was confident or foolish enough to believe that I could transport Judy faster to the hospital than waiting for EMT personnel to arrive.

I wouldn't recommend this course of action.

Whether that was the correct decision or not, I went with

my gut in the moment. I quickly grabbed our rolling desk chair and with Judy still in her urine-soaked clothes, I lifted her into the chair, pushed her through our apartment, into the garage and transferred her into the car seat. It is amazing how with adrenaline surging through your body, you're able to be in full active motion before the mind has the full ability to catch up.

What seemed like an unfathomable amount of time had only been minutes from reacting to Judy on the bedroom floor to reversing our car down the driveway and hastily being on our way. Thankfully, traffic was extremely scarce this early in the morning and I took advantage of the lack of roadway competition to transport Judy to Mercy Hospital as our emergency destination with speeds higher than the advertised limit. Even though it was only a few miles from our driveway to the Emergency Department (ED) doors, each mile brought a fresh wave of panic, fearful urgency, and silent pleading/demanding prayers. *"God, this can't be it!" "God, we need You!" "You've got to do something!" "We need Your help!"* For Judy's sake, I kept the emotional roller coaster and prayerful appeals to myself. Taking quick glances at Judy, I knew that her emotional state hinged on mine, so I fought to keep my composure for as long she was by my side.

I'm not sure why I chose Mercy Hospital as the location for this unfolding trauma. Neither Judy nor I had any prior experiences or encounters with Mercy that drew me there. There was nothing special in my mind that immediately screamed, "MERCY." It wasn't even the closest hospital in proximity to where we lived. In fact, I had to pass another hospital, which I'm sure was a qualified medical facility, in order to get to Mercy. But whatever instinctual impulse or God-given directive sent my way, Mercy was my choice. Once the decision was made, there was no other option.

Darkness still hung over the early morning as I pulled into the Mercy Hospital cul-du-sac. The light of the sun wouldn't break through the night's hold for another couple of hours.

Darkness' grip seemed so poignantly compatible to the anxiety and desperation that hung over my emotions. In contrast to the night sky, the Emergency Department (ED) loading zone was brightly illuminated. The high intensity LED white "EMER-GENCY" lettering shone like a beacon, providing the target I was aiming for. Having no clue where I was supposed to go in this moment, I located the closest open spot I could find and parked the car with the blinkers flashing. I'm absolutely certain that I was in a restricted, "No Parking" zone. I didn't think twice. It didn't matter. As I ran towards the ED entrance, COVID restrictions greeted me with yellow caution tape and orange cones directing me to a folding table with a dimly lit sign the read, "Check in Here" outside the ED entrance. Behind the table were two ED staff who were clearly not ready for the verbal intensity that was about to come their way. Before I even reached the table, I yelled, *"My wife's had a stroke!" "She's in the car right there!"* Pointing to the inappropriately parked vehicle with the lights flashing. I loudly repeated, *"She's had a stroke!"*

Without hesitation, the ED staffer voiced over his radio, *"Stroke alert! ED entrance. Patient vehicle. Stroke Alert!"* The staffer had barely taken a post announcement breath when a team of emergency personnel rapidly emerged from the ED doors with a gurney in tow. Appearing much like an Olympic bobsled team, each member was evenly spaced along both sides of the gurney, running at a full clip with precision and focused determination. Upon reaching the car, Judy was carefully but forcibly extracted from our Honda Fit, placed on the gurney and hurried back inside, disappearing behind the ED sliding glass doors. The rush took only a matter of precious seconds.

The night air was silent again. I stood alone. The intensity of the situation had moved inside with numerous calculated and well-trained procedural steps beginning to unfold. With Judy now out of sight, I slipped into the driver's seat, clutched the steering wheel with both hands and a river of tears was unleashed. These would be the first of many to come.

* * *

I first had the pleasure of meeting Judy Burling at St. Paul Bible College (now Crown College). I was a "wet-behind-the-ears" young, naïve freshman. Judy, on the other hand, was a well-established, more mature upper classman on campus. St. Paul Bible College, or SPBC as it was affectionately called, is a 215-acre beautiful, rural campus located about an hour west of Minneapolis, MN with an enrollment of less than a thousand on-campus students at the time. This small, private, Christian college was an ideal match for this introverted, quiet, insecure city boy from Des Moines, Iowa.

I grew up in a loving, stable, middle-class family. My dad was a devoted, kind, and hardworking self-employed CPA. While he was generally quiet and soft spoken, rarely raising his voice or expressing emotion, my older sister, Marjean, and I never doubted his love and care for us. My mom was the quintessential stay-at-home wife/mom of that era. She worked tirelessly making sure that our small family of four had what we needed each and every day. Mom prepared and cooked every single meal, instilling in us the important family value of being present around the dinner table every evening. It wasn't optional no matter how old were. Family meant sitting at a table and sharing a meal together. Both of my parents also ingrained in my sister and I the value of church and faith. Neither of them was outspoken or demonstrative in proclaiming their faith or engaged in much discussion about it but they modeled its importance and the necessity of regular church attendance... whether I wanted to go or not. No matter how old I was.

Just like being present at the family dinner table wasn't optional, neither was going to church. If the church was open, we were there. Sunday morning, Sunday night, and Wednesday night. If the doors were open, we would be in a pew. Part of that was because a primary element of my mom's theology and belief in God was wrapped around the notion that if we didn't go to church there would be a negative consequence which would be directly tied to the fact that God was punishing us. This cause and effect was due to the correlation in her mind that the traumatic, unexpected, disheartening and disappointing interruptions of life, most likely, equaled God's punishment. My mom, unfortunately, carried that heavy-handed view of God throughout her life.

For me, however, growing up attending church with that underlying view of God created some deep confusion. I believed, or wanted to believe, that God loved me but the conflicting belief which ran vehemently within me was that the unexpectedly grievous and traumatic events that punctuate our lives are inextricably linked to God's punishment for having done something wrong. Which, if that's true, then the only conclusion I could arrive at was that God didn't really care about me. God was, in a sense, a purely harsh disciplinarian. The corrosive nature of that conclusion had a damaging impact on me and left me struggling to grasp how God could be good and loving and yet, so punitive and uncaring. It was this internal struggle that made me extremely open to the Bible College environment and hungry for the courses I was about to undertake. I desperately needed to resolve this theological and internal conflict. As a young man having felt called to full-time pastoral ministry, it was time to dive in and find out who I was and what I truly believed about this God I had placed my faith in. The resolution to this conflict would, interestingly, not come from any Bible College classroom but from the church that Judy and I would later attend.

Judy, like myself, also grew up in a secure, middle-class family in the heart of Wisconsin. Both her parents were hardworking, responsible, salt-of-the-earth individuals who were determined to provide for their family. Being one of four children, Judy learned early on that to be heard, it would be necessary to speak up and engage in conversation. This created some lively, spirited, and, at times, passionate discussions around the

Burling household. Quite the contrast from my quieter, restrained upbringing. Certainly not better or worse, just different. But I'm so thankful for the difference because it helped create the Judy that I came to love. While Judy's family were regular church goers, it wasn't until she went to a Christian young adult conference as a sophomore attending a university in Wisconsin that she fully came alive to faith in God. The quest for personal meaning that had been missing in her life was now fulfilled in Jesus. This radical spiritual change prompted her to pursue transferring from the university she had been attending to a Bible college. After scouring through the university's guidance counselor's library, she came across a dust covered, archaic academic catalog for SPBC. Upon opening it and surveying what SPBC offered, it was like Heaven opened and Judy knew without a doubt that that was her new spiritual and higher education destination. The decision to transfer was made. I couldn't be more grateful for that dust covered archaic, hidden gem of a catalog buried between so much other reading material.

It caught Judy's eye. Therefore, it caused our paths to cross and a love story to unfold. God knew.

On campus, Judy and I were quite different.

She was extroverted, I was introverted.

She was animated. I was restrained.

She talked. I listened.

She was socially active. I was socially awkward.

She had dated. I was the proud owner of one date my entire life. In fact, when I met Judy, she was coming off a heart-wrenching breakup from a serious relationship that had lasted two years. On the other hand, I was clueless about what a breakup was or how one even felt.

While Judy had caught my attention in the hallways, chapels, and cafeteria, it wasn't until we were partnered together on an intermural volleyball team that I found the courage to go against my introverted nature and verbally engage with this 5'2" wonder with the most amazingly clear blue eyes. We laughed more than we were contributors on the volleyball court. Thankfully, no one on our team took their volleyball skills or the score very competitively. Which gave room for Judy and me to revel in each other's company without the pressure of letting our team down. Her quick wit and quicker humor, her ability to not take herself too seriously, and her deeply committed walk with Jesus instantly captivated me. I found myself strategically intersecting with her throughout the day for the purpose of snagging a few brief moments between classes to catch up with her. Having discovered that she was a part-time receptionist in the Registrar's Office, I frequently "*needed*" to visit the Registrar's Office even though I didn't have any registration issues. My course schedule was just fine. I was truthfully creating stealthy moments to steal glimpses of Judy's beautiful face. Without acknowledging it, I believe Judy caught on to my subtle scheme rather quickly.

I was more comfortable around her than with anyone ever before in my life.

We had our official first date on a biting cold Minnesota evening in January as we celebrated a friend's birthday. That was the genesis of a blossoming romance. The following Sunday, given that we were dutiful Bible College students, Judy invited me to attend church with her. With the church we were going to attend being forty-five minutes away from campus, I volunteered to drive and arranged to pick her up outside her dorm. Parking my 1980 white Monte Carlo at the end of the sidewalk extending from Judy's dorm, I waited only a few seconds until she came enthusiastically bounding out the door making her way towards me. As she approached the car, she suddenly disappeared from view having slipped on the icy pavement. Instantly, she sprang back to her feet. Opening the car door, she stated matter-of-factly and without hesitation, "I'm fine. Good to go." Two profound facts struck me at that moment. One, never again would I fail to get out and open the door for her. Secondly, I knew that Judy was the one for me. She was a "bounce backer-upper." This momentary incident symbolized her tenacity to not allow herself to stay down. She was a mountain of determination hidden within a 5'2" frame. So confident was I in knowing Judy was the one for me that I wrote a letter home to my parents expressing the capturing of my heart by a certain young woman. Thinking back on that letter now, I'm sure my parents were shocked and dismayed by my aggressive certainty. No matter, I wanted them to know. Everything was beautifully perfect. Or… so I thought. Bible College can tend to create not-so-realistic views on romance and relationships.

As it turned out, while my confidence about Judy was soaring, she was not so certain about me. Questions lingered in her mind and other options still presented themselves as competitors to my affections, which she needed to consider. So as the roller coaster of relationships go, Judy broke up with me. Not once but three times! I never broke up with her. Break up score…Eric 0; Judy 3. I'm just stating the facts. I was forced to drink the bitter water of heartache. But it wasn't just that she broke up with me, it was the timing of the breakups that pierced my heart with cruel and unusual punishment. The first time was at the beginning of the Fall school year. We had both just returned to campus after a summer separated by long distance at a time when FaceTime or video messaging weren't available for hearts aflame like ours. Our only means of connection was a rotary phone. It was the dark ages. So, returning to campus and being back together in person carried expectant hopes for the coming year. Regardless, high expectations crushed.

The second time was right before finals week. Needless to say, those finals tanked.

The trifecta of heartache happened right before summer break of the same school year. But what made the third time so much more gut-wrenching was that I had rented an apartment and found a job in the Minneapolis area for the summer. I forfeited going back home and arranged to stay in the same location where Judy was living because the plan…that we previously agreed on…was that by me living in close proximity to her, we'd have a wonderful, eventful summer together. It was going to be great. Except, instead, all I got was heartache. Unfortunately, because Judy was the only person I knew in Minneapolis that summer, I just kept showing up at her door…even though we were broken up. Like a lost puppy that had nowhere else to go, I would end up on Judy's doorstep, *hungry and lonely hoping for a morsel of affection.*

As painful as those breakups were for me, they offered Judy the necessary time to hear the convincing words from God that she was seeking, "Eric's the one for you. It's ok to choose him." Once that was confirmed for her, there was no going back or questioning anymore. We were now a couple committed to a future trajectory. Judy understood me, she challenged me to spiritually grow and to unswervingly know my calling, and she loved me even with all my Iowa quirks and sense of humor. On the other hand, I got Judy. I appreciated and strongly admired her passion to make sure that others were known and seen. I loved her smile and how it was a deeper expression of her love for life. Most of all, I understood Judy as a woman who valued authenticity, humility, sincerity, and positivity. She was undoubtedly a woman who honestly spoke her mind.

Five months later, having dated for close to two years, I knew it was time to ask Judy the all-important question. God had led us so far since those first evening intramural volleyball games. Even though we were young, we felt ready for the adventure ahead. I was more certain than ever that Judy was the one for me. Living frugally for months, I saved enough of my meager income to purchase a ring. The first big, personal purchase of my life. The weightiness of the investment was not lost on me. This ring would symbolize a narrative of love, commitment, forgiveness, and patience about to be penned with all of heaven as a witness. Following spending Christmas with my family, I jumped in my car on December 26 and drove the 362 miles from Des Moines, IA to Ripon, WI. Rehearsing my proposal presentation the entire length of the trip. I wanted it to be meaningful and memorable. Arriving at Judy's parent's home, my nerves got the better of me and I wasted little time popping the question. I did absolutely nothing to create a memorable, romantic vibe. No fanfare. No setting up the moment. No "can I have everyone's attention." But it was *memorable*. The TV was blaring, Judy's dad was reading the newspaper, and her sister, Nancy, reclining on a living room chair, was unknowingly watching whatever program was airing. In this *romantic, fairytale moment* (sarcasm intended), I blundered through asking for Bob's permission to marry his daughter which I don't think he fully understood what was being asked of him through my nervous mumbling. Without pausing to receive his answer, I proceeded to pull the tiny box containing the ring from the present I had skillfully disguised it in. It was now, at this poignant, enchanting juncture in time that Bob and Nancy caught on to the scene unfolding in their living room and their attention shifted in Judy and I's direction. With Judy's exuberant and affirmative answer to my question, we all erupted in cheers and hugs. It was truly a significant moment. Until we realized that the whole event had transpired without her mom being home to witness it. Marge was at the store. When she arrived home a few minutes later, we all recreated the whole proposal a second time for Marge's benefit as if it was the first go around. It was *magical*. Truthfully, it was an exact representation of our relationship. Unpretentious, unflamboyant, heartfelt, sincere, humorous and full of grace.

With the engagement secure, the next six months were a whirlwind of planning, pre-marital counseling, and me finishing my collegiate junior year. Judy, having graduated the previous spring, was now working full time in the Registrar's Office. While I never married for money, her working full time in a campus staff capacity would prove to be, of sorts, a financial windfall for me. You see, by me marrying a full time SPBC staff member, I was given the "married staff" benefit of not owing anything for my upcoming senior year of college. So, in a way, I hit the mother lode. I was going to marry Judy and get my last year tuition free. Judy was also living off campus in an apartment above the residence of one of our professors. That small apartment would become our first home and contain cherished memories. But for now, that apartment was "planning central." All the details and decisions necessary to coordinate the wedding of our dreams were determined in that tiny space. With Church of the Open Door, located in a northern suburb of Minneapolis, being our home church, Judy and I knew of no sweeter place we wanted to gather with family and friends and celebrate the joining of our lives together than there. The sanctuary with its beautifully peaked ceiling, large, centered wooden cross, and pleasing ambiance offered the perfect setting that we desired. This was more than building. It was home.

Church of the Open Door is one of those milestone markers on my roadmap of life. For both Judy and me, Open Door was where our spiritual walk with Jesus found traction and our eyes and hearts were fully opened to a relationship with Him, forever changing who Judy and I would become. But more significantly for me, it was at Open Door and under the teaching of the Lead Pastor, David Johnson, that I encountered the beautiful truth of God's grace. Even though I had grown up religiously attending church, grace was an unknown and foreign concept. It was grace that started my internal conflict resolution that I previously mentioned. It was this introduction to grace that launched my theological recovery with the fresh understanding that God, while being a loving father who disciplines those He loves, is not a harsh, uncaring punisher. He is not looking to crush but rather to restore and who continually invites us to come home into his outstretched arms of love. Through the grace of God, my value and worth are settled. He wants me! This was revolutionary to my spiritual thinking. So it was in this community that Judy and I encountered deep Biblical teaching and passionate worship in ways that impacted and marked us from that season forward. The Bible became more than a book, it became a living, breathing entity that breathed life into our spiritual lungs. Desperately wanting Pastor Dave to perform the ceremony, we catered our wedding date to his schedule. Once his availability was confirmed, it was all systems go.

The afternoon of July 13, 1985, was unseasonably hot and humid for Minnesota. With the temperature hovering near 100 sweltering degrees and the humidity causing everything to wilt and perspiration to bead on everyone's foreheads, family and friends filed into that sacred space with celebratory anticipation. As our guests arrived, Judy and I knew that this was about more than simply an obligatory wedding. There was a clear purpose for this moment in time. Divine intentionality to not only celebrate the joining of two lives into one but to also joyfully celebrate the One who had brought those lives together. Judy and I wanted our wedding ceremony to be a wonderful, worshipful testimony of the work of God in us and the New Testament book of Ephesians would provide the context.

Despite the heat, Judy was radiantly wearing a cream floor length gown with a stunning train, scoop neckline, and long sleeves. With her hair perfectly permed and her head adorned with a bridal veil wreath, she was absolutely beautiful. I, looking more like a nervous teenager than a soon-to-be-married man in his early 20's, wore a cream tuxedo with tails and a rose silk cummerbund. Our wedding party, comprised of Judy's sisters and dear friends, elegantly matched the chosen colors. As the ceremony began, the poetic language from the Apostle Paul set the stage, "he predestined us for adoption to sonship through Jesus Christ, in accordance with his pleasure and will—to the praise of his glorious grace, which he has freely given us in the One he loves" (Ephesians 1:5-6 NIV). We invited God's grace, freely given to us through Jesus Christ, to be the unshakeable bedrock of our marriage. In those ceremonial moments, Judy and I had no idea how much that bedrock of grace would be called upon for strength in the years to come.

Pastor Dave spoke on the reality of living in a society where

selfishness, entitlement, and unhealthy expectations are so preva-
lent in relationships and marriages but how that wasn't God's
original design. God's design for marriage wasn't for Judy and
me to find our security and significance in each other or that the
one we're joining our life to be held solely responsible to meet all
of our selfish needs. But rather, only God alone, through His
grace, is the One who can offer true security, value, and significance and be able to meet us in our crucible of needs. Pastor
Dave's challenges were that in the inevitability of mistakes, be
quick to forgive, in the light of God's love, love each other
deeply, and that our life together be prayerfully marked by
humility, honesty, an enormous capacity for patience, heaven-
sent grace, laughter, and that we would "know the hope to
which he (GOD) has called us, the riches of his glorious inheritance in his holy people" (Ephesians 1:18 NIV). Being in our
early 20's, neither Judy nor I had much real exposure to life's
demands. We were wide-eyed, naïvely optimistic young lovers
eagerly anticipating a honeymoon, completely oblivious to the
pressure cooker that life could be and the immense testing that
would come our way. But we fully committed ourselves to the
vows presented to us:

"I, Eric, take you, Judy, to be my wedded wife."
"To have and to hold from this day forward."
"For better, for worse."
"For richer, for poorer."
"To love and to cherish."
"In sickness and in health."
"Till death due us part."

* * *

Having found a more legal, long term parking space, I raced
back to the Emergency Department and anxiously waited in line
to be admitted by security through the imposing double doors

that separated the world from the ED inner sanctum. The ED was, unfortunately, a zoo on this early morning. Every type of humanity with every assortment of symptoms and injuries filled the waiting room and the admittance line. The anguish, despair, and agony etched on the faces was a blunt reminder of how fragile human life is. We often believe we're impenetrable, unstoppable, and unbreakable especially when we're young. But the coughs, cries, and pleas for help were a clear reminder that that is anything but true. Peter's sobering statement about human frailty caught me in this moment, "People are like grass; their beauty is like a flower in the field. The grass withers and the flower fades" (1 Peter 1:24 NLT). We are a mixture of fragility and strength with no ability to fully control either. We are definitely not as strong as we think we are. We grasp and clutch, trying to hang onto youthful vigor and vitality. We do all we can to avoid or at least detain the inevitable process of aging or the sudden invasion of trauma but it finds us anyway. Therefore, there has to be more that we anchor our life to than our own efforts. Life is meant to be more than groveling after the dust of the ground hoping beyond hope to unearth a sense of significance, value, identity, and worth. That ED waiting room admonished me with the reality that while life is fleeting, there is more available to us, even in the midst of extreme chaos and uncertainty through the assurance of God's grace.

Even though the waiting in line was probably only a few minutes, it felt like everything was moving at a snail's pace. The security officer's questions, the person's responses, the RN's and nurses' aides moving people to the next station or to an empty chair so that the following person in line could repeat the process all over again were all excruciatingly slow. I was growing more and more impatient. I just wanted to get to Judy. I could feel the adrenaline surging through my nervous system as if I had consumed way too many cups of overly caffeinated coffee. When it was finally my turn I didn't wait for the rehearsed questions before I blurted out that I needed to find my wife. "She just came in with a possible stroke! I need to know what room she's in!" This was obviously not the security officer's first night on duty as he calmly asked me, "What's her name?" I'm sure he'd seen his fair share before of panic-stricken spouses acting as if their traumatic crisis trumped all others. "Judy Foust. She was just brought in." As the officer checked his computer monitors for evidence of Judy's whereabouts, he asked me, "What's your name? And how are you related?" I answered rather emphatically, "I'm Eric Foust. I'm her husband." Once confirmed, I was escorted by a different security officer passed the double doors and through the corridors to ED Room #5. There I found Judy already attached to monitors recording her blood pressure, heart rate, oxygen levels, and temperature.

Seeing Judy in this condition pulled heavy on my heart. When I asked her how she was doing, she reassuringly replied, "I'm ok." Leaning over the gurney railing, I cupped her face in my hands, looked intently into her eyes and responded back, "You're doing great. There's nothing to worry about." I'm pretty sure I said that last optimistic statement for my benefit more than Judy's. While there was a slight left side facial droop and her speech was also slightly slurred, I felt some relief in noticing that her condition didn't appear to be as bad as I initially thought. She was alert, responsive, talkative, and seemed to be only minimally affected by the night's traumatic ordeal. As the chaos of the ED enveloped the boundaries outside of ED Room #5, everything within ED Room #5 was refined to a singular focus. The monitor alarms and bells from neighboring ED rooms, EMT arrivals, medical conversations, the sounds of hurried medical equipment, and hospital notifications being broadcast over the intercom system became an indistinguishable cacophony of noise that lost all relevance inside ED Room #5. I simple sat fixated on the methodical hum of the blood pressure cuff as it regularly inflated and released on Judy's arm revealing new systolic and diastolic readings on the screen while she drifted in and out of sleep. It was comforting to see her peacefully sleep as every rise and fall of her chest with every inhale and exhale made the unnormal environment feel a little more normal. That sleep, however, was purposefully interrupted by phlebotomists needing to take a blood draw and RN's regularly checking Judy's vitals. Each time that she was startled awake, Judy's nurse would kindly apologize for the disturbance to which Judy would respond with equal kindness, "It's ok. You're doing a good job." Even here, in ED Room #5, where selfishness and self-preoccupation would not be out of the norm and certainly understandable, Judy was still concerned with making sure that those around her were encouraged.

At approximately 7:30am, the attending Emergency Physician, Dr. O'Brien, came into our room updating us on the situation and informing us that, per stroke protocol, an MRI was scheduled for within the hour. I'm not sure why but medical abbreviations have always seemed intimidating and more concerning for me in comparison to what they stand for. MRI, CT scan, EKG, CVA, DVT, UTI and Echo all seem to communicate a foreign language that is wrapped in mystery and intrigue. As if the persons using those abbreviations are trying to spell something in code for my own safety and ignorance. It wasn't long, however, before the medical imaging team appeared, introduced themselves and informed Judy and me again of the upcoming procedure, then briskly disconnected Judy from her electronic monitors and whisked her away. ED Room #5 was quiet. With Judy and her gurney no longer present, the space seemed larger, eerily empty. Monitor cables hung harmlessly towards the floor. The machine screen which before was continuously tracking heart rates and breathing patterns was now motionless with only the last recorded blood pressure numbers frozen in view. Humanity was still in full motion outside those walls but inside it felt cold, void, and lifeless.

With the only piece of regulation hospital equipment left in the room being the folding chair I was sitting on, I leaned back, rested my head on the wall behind me and closed my eyes. The emotional ebb and flow of the last hours had been exhausting. I sighed deeply in an attempt to release some of the inner tension and anxiety that had built up. In that moment of solitude as the turbulence in my mind began to briefly settle, I recalled the words of Genesis 1 where it states so clearly that you and I, we're made, we're created in the image of God. Which means that we have characteristics, emotions and identity features that are similar to God all wrapped up in this physical, earthly container of a body. But I think that there's something that we often forget when it comes to this truth about being created in the image of God and that is that we're made and created *by* God. He formed us. He made us.

Now I can hear the wheels in your mind turning even as you're reading this, "No, I was made because mom and dad decided to '*wrestle*' and miraculously cells joined together ultimately producing this physical body that we have to live with." I understand that and it's true. But that does not remove the fact that God has stamped His image in us. There is an intrinsic value about us because we have been made, created, and designed by God. We bear His image. Judy, even in her tenuous physical condition and being wheeled through the hospital hallways for a magnetic resonance imaging scan, still bore the unshakeable image of God. It was stamped in her and hadn't diminished one bit. It was just as vibrant and whole and priceless as the day she was born. But to take this one step further in this thought processing together, because we are made in the image of God…

…because God is great and doesn't do anything halfway…

…because God has never designed or done anything with the attitude of, "Eh, that's good enough" …

…but because everything God does is done from the greatness of His God-ness, that means that God did not put average in us!

We are not a sub-standard, mediocre version of His image. We are created in His image, out of His greatness, for a purpose.

Which means that, hear this again, we are of immense value. I wish I could edit that over so many of the recordings that might be running through your mind pertaining to your personal sense of worth. You are not sub-par. You are not average. You are not mediocre when it comes to God's design and calling on your life. It is so grievous that for so many, the statements of a flawed parent, the consequences of an event or a poor decision, or the insults and comments of an individual who didn't actually know you have done more to cement your identity than the God who's image you bear and who, according to the Psalmist, fearfully and wonderfully made you. Judy was, in this moment, still fearfully and wonderfully made even though her body and mind were not fully cooperating in alignment with this truth. Realizing afresh that Judy was made, created, and designed by God, which meant that He knew her, brought a faint sense of comfort to my weary soul. It was a small gift of peace. God was not unavailable in nor unaware of our traumatic chaos.

After forty-five minutes, Judy returned looking even more exhausted from her MRI excursion but no less engaging. As the technicians maneuvered her gurney back into its position in the room, she said to me, "Good, you're still here. I didn't want you to leave." There was nowhere else in the world I was going to be than in ED #5 waiting for her. She was my world. Then, with her quick wit still intact she quipped, "And they didn't lose me either" as she tilted her head to catch a smile from her handlers.

As Judy drifted off to sleep while we waited for Dr. O'Brien to share with us the results of the MRI, I began the imperative task of communicating Judy's circumstances to family and close friends. I first notified our kids, Erika, Joel, and Seth and their spouses about their mom's situation. Being a close family that is spread across the US, I knew that this text would disrupt their worlds. As their days were all moving forward at different speeds and junctures given their time zones, this news was going to hit with jarring abruptness. After our kids, I texted Judy's work team letting them know that she had had a possible stroke and that I'd keep them updated with any changes throughout the day. Gabe, Holly, and Stephen meant so much to Judy and so I wanted them to know of her condition with honesty and urgency. For Judy, her work crew was almost as much like family as her own children. They are definitely a part of our community. As the hours passed, I continued my mission to spread the word to as many family members and close friends as I thought needed to know. I fully believed that another text regarding Judy's physical plight lighting up a screen on a friend's phone was one more invitation to join me in interceding for Judy and her recovery. Hoping that by flooding the throne room of heaven in prayer, it would move God to respond sooner and more aggressively on Judy's behalf. As often as I was pressing the "send" arrow with my text message, my phone was vibrating in response with expressions of sympathy and prayer. While physically unseen, there was a groundswell of support forming Judy's team.

The day crept along with absurd slowness but eventually Dr. O'Brien appeared with some initial results from the morning's tests. Trying to keep the medical language to an understandable vocabulary for us, he stated that the MRI showed evidence of multiple subacute infarcts in the brain. Further watering down the language to an even more understandable level, he described how a subacute infarction is a recent onset condition caused by a blockage in a blood vessel in the brain. He also informed us that per stroke evaluation protocol, a chest x-ray had been taken but showed no evidence of pulmonary or heart abnormalities. Dr. O'Brien further explained to us that CT scans of Judy's head and neck had also been performed which did reveal a significant concern as she was found to have complete occlusion or blockage on the right carotid artery and the left carotid artery was 80%-90% stenotic. Again, sensing any lack of medical comprehension registering on my face, he redefined his previous statement by saying that the left carotid artery, while not occluded, was showing an 80%-90% narrowing of that partic- ular artery. With that information regarding Judy's brain, my brain felt overwhelmed and overloaded. Given the situation, he recommended that Judy be admitted and kept overnight for further stroke work-up and be re-evaluated in the morning.

From all appearances, Judy looked to have come through her ordeal relatively unscathed. She was smiling, communicating clearly and understandably with complete sentences, and was attentive, as usual, to all the medical staff coming in and out of her space. Not a single Dr., RN, or aide who came within eyesight of Judy wasn't asked what their name was. Judy needed to know. For Judy, names hold significant value. She has always been much better than me at remembering names. I can recall a face but remembering names is out of my league. Name remembrance was of second nature to Judy. Which had proven, over and over, to be an invaluable asset to me through the years as we served in church ministry together. She bailed me out of countless potential horrendous situations by recalling a person's name before I bungled my way through the embarrassment of not knowing a name that I should have.

But for Judy, knowing your name carried deeper significance. Judy knowing your name meant that you mattered to her and she wanted you to know that. You weren't simply a random person intersecting with her on the pathway of life. If she was going to look you in the face, then knowing the name that went with that face was of utmost importance. In a culture that can so easily hide behind social media platforms and avoid personal connection and in a society that can rush through life with our heads down, never fixing our gaze on or making eye contact with another individual thereby rendering us detached, isolated, and impersonal, Judy, with everything about her, fought to be the antithesis of those cultural and societal trends. Our church teaching experience has taught us that names mattered in the Bible. When God gave a person a name, there was purpose, identity and a mission attached to that name. Names weren't frivolously tossed around but intentionally etched by God into the fabric of the person's soul. Moses, Noah, Abraham, Isaac, and Jacob for example weren't simply names for prominent characters in the Old Testament, they were identities that defined their purposes. Most importantly, the same is true of Jesus. Jesus wasn't just his name, it defined his purpose for stepping into the timeline of humanity. The angel from God said to Mary, "you are to name him **Jesus**, for he will save his people from their sins" (Matthew 1:21 NIV). For God, names mattered. They instilled identity and value. For Judy, names mattered.

With Judy settled in her room and me being exhausted and on the docket to preach at both our Sunday gatherings in a couple of days, I went home to sleep with the reassurance that Judy would be well taken care of overnight. While sleep was spotty and often interrupted with the unnerving realization that Judy was absent from our bed, the few consistent moments of rest helped me feel somewhat refreshed.

Visiting hours began at 8:00am and having promised Judy that I would be there as soon as visitors were allowed entrance, I was back at the hospital at 8:00am on Saturday morning, Sept 4 with a fresh set of clothes for her and hopeful optimism. As I walked into the room, Judy gave me a huge, welcoming Judy smile. Shortly after arriving, breakfast was delivered. The floor nurse indicated that having had an initial morning conversation with the Dr. that Judy had improved enough overnight and that if she cleared a few hurdles that morning, she could possibly be discharged that afternoon. This was incredibly encouraging news after the previous day's ordeal. Judy's first hurdle in being declared able to be discharged was to satisfactorily eat her breakfast which she did with ease. Regardless of the culinary quality, she ate a significant amount and called it good. The second hurdle was to succeed at using the bathroom under her own power. Again, she cleared that hurdle with flying colors. The third hurdle was the most strenuous and demanding of the three. Judy would need to walk the hallway under the careful watch of a physical therapist.

The physical therapist appeared with a walker in hand. The

objective would be for Judy to stand on her own strength, stabilize herself using the walker and stroll down the hallway as far as the therapist deemed necessary and back again. With the instructions out of the way, the therapist firmly placed the walker directly in front of Judy as she sat on the edge of the bed and said, "Let's go." I tentatively and anxiously watched as Judy assertively grabbed the arms of the walker and lifted herself up to a standing position with hardly any effort at all. It was like she was climbing out of bed the same way she had done every other morning for the past 61 years of her life…minus the walker. Easy. Once the therapist was confident that Judy was stable, she gave the all-clear to walk. With the therapist next to Judy as a precautionary measure to catch her if she started to topple over, Judy lifted and reset the walker on the floor several inches in front of her and took her first steps. The two repeated this process a couple more times until Judy moved beyond the door-frame and into the hallway. In the hallway with a clear path in front of her, Judy took steps forward again with relative ease. The walker was actually more of a hindrance than a help to Judy's forward progress so the therapist removed the walker from Judy's grip and carried it the rest of the journey while Judy walked free and upright. It was a beautiful and emotionally relieving sight. Judy was walking physically unobstructed as if she were taking a casual jaunt with a friend. I choked up on the spot. Her left upper extremity strength was graded as 4/5 and she had walked without assistance. She passed! Judy would be coming home. After 30 hours of high intensity drama, Judy would be coming home ready to resume normal life again. Our nightmare was over.

Little did I know at the time that these steps would be some of the last that Judy would take.

Around noon, Dr. O'Brien, Dr. Alvarez and the floor nurse arrived with discharge instructions. Dr. O'Brien reported that the physical therapist had concluded that Judy was doing quite well from a physical therapy standpoint and didn't see any need to order the use of a walker at home. She did, however, recommend that Judy continue with some minor outpatient physical, occupational, and speech therapy in order to counteract any lingering stroke affects. Dr. O'Brien further discussed potential warning signs that we should watch for in case of a reoccurrence at home and informed us that he had made a referral to Dr. Erek Helseth, a vascular neurology specialist, regarding Judy's left carotid stenosis. Other than that, the only other instructions given were to start her on a new daily medication regimen that included Plavix, aspirin, and a statin. This regimen would last for 3 months at which time, Judy should have a follow up appointment with her primary doctor and Dr. Helseth to monitor her progress or any changes. As the doctors exited the room, the nurse pulled me aside and exhortingly told me not to hesitate to call if I noticed any changes or relapse in Judy's condition. He even gave me his personal cell phone number to call should I have any concerns or questions over the next day or two.

With the discharge instructions all taken care of and the necessary discharge paperwork in hand, Judy was given the greenlight to get dressed and go home. In only a few minutes, Judy was ready to leave and, for precautionary measures, was wheeled out of the hospital by a member of the nursing staff. As I pulled our car up to meet them in the pick-up lane at the visitor/outpatient doors, I thanked God for the protective, healing work that He had done on Judy's behalf. My wife was coming home and for that I could not have been more grateful. A serious life-threatening situation had been resolved without any recognizable deficit or loss in Judy's physical body. At the car, she joyfully transferred from the wheelchair to the car seat and we were on our way. We were free! Homeward bound. Those few miles from hospital to home were some of the most beautiful miles I've ever driven. Now, thinking back on that moment of thankful prayer in the pick-up lane and traveling those few beautiful miles home, I'm brought up short by how quickly my prayers are determined by and forged out of my temporary changing circumstances rather than by my unshakeable faith in my permanently unchangeable God. Less than thirty-six hours earlier, I was driving those same few miles pleading with and demanding God to do something, anything, but be silent and inactive for Judy's sake and the apparent wrongness of what was unfolding. Not that I was necessarily questioning God's goodness in that early morning hour but I was certainly calling into question His care and concern. But then thirty-six hours later, I'm thanking God for His goodness, care, protection, and everything being right in our lives again because of our improved circumstances. I don't say this out of guilt or that it was even spiritually wrong on my part to voice such polar opposite prayers to my Father in heaven. In fact, I think it's predictably normal to pray with such extremely opposite intentions knowing that our God understands and offers grace amid life's uncertainties. He knows our frailties, our fragileness, our emotional swings, our temper tantrums, our joyous, relieved, happy outbursts and loves us through it all. He invites us by faith to step out of the boat in raging waters and catches us when our perspective and focus wanes amidst the torrent around us and we begin to sink. It is what He does so mercifully. But it saddens me that my heart and faith can be so fickle in the crucible of uncontrollable and unwanted life interruptions so as to push the pendulum swing of my prayers to such opposite lengths.

Having not slept much during her stay in the hospital, the first thing Judy wanted to do once arriving home was to take a nap. Yes! A nap! I totally understood her desire to rest and was more than willing to do the same. Judy laid down and comfortably positioned herself on our sofa and I tenderly covered her with a blanket, again thankful that she was home. In only a matter of minutes, Judy was soundly asleep. In the quiet of *our* living room, I simply sat and listened to her gentle breathing, gazed on her peaceful face which was home for me, and reflected on this life that we had made together. We had much to be thankful for and had been blessed in more ways than we could ever recount. Trials and hardships had certainly frequented our thirty-six years of marriage, but we had been blessed. We could celebrate having three amazing kids, Erika, Joel, and Seth. All, in spite of their parents' share of flaws and quirks, had grown into confident, independent, character filled adults who married spouses, Tim, Victoria, and Ashlynne who Judy and I couldn't be more proud of. With our immediate family expanding to now include four grandchildren, we deeply and truly loved what the Foust family had become and was becoming. I found myself resonating with the Psalmist who wrote, "Children born to a young man are like arrows in a warrior's hands. How joyful is a man whose quiver is full of them! He will not be put to shame when he confronts his accusers at the city gates" (Psalm 127:4-5). In the stillness, safety, and comfort surrounding me, I sat and stared for several more minutes at this wonderful individual that I had spent well over half my life with and then drifted off to sleep myself.

At a little past 2:00pm, I awoke and found Judy still deep in sleep. Not wanting to disturb her, I quietly gathered her hospital clothing, her soiled pajama clothes from two nights before and put them all in the washing machine. I can humbly admit that while I know how to effectively and successfully handle a load of laundry, Judy has primarily been the one to oversee this important task in the past. Not because of some agreed upon marital duty or responsibility or because of a wrongly assumed outdated anti-feminist requirement, but simply because Judy found delight in doing the laundry and doing it well. But frequently, I would jump in and wash a load, albeit, without the same level of color separation and care. Sometimes, the results of my handiwork were quite noticeable. Truthfully, Judy had an engrained work ethic that was very evident around our home. When it came to cleaning, there were no shortcuts and I was adamantly instructed on what proper cleaning and house cleanliness looked like. While I was not always a compliant student nor always amenable to the ways of the teacher, over time I came to value the eradication of carpet dirt, grime, build-up, piles of dirty laundry, and a sink full of dishes as much as Judy.

Having been asleep now for nearly two hours and feeling uneasy about letting her sleep for any longer duration of time, I gently awakened Judy at 3:00pm. As Judy slowly came to her senses, I immediately knew she wasn't right. As if a forceful, direct blow had landed to my chest knocking the wind out of me, I found it difficult to inhale and catch my breath. With each quick attempted burst of inhalation to fill my lungs, the seriousness of the situation penetrated even deeper. We had immediately been thrown into turbulent waters once again. The left side of Judy's face displayed extreme left sided paresthesia or left side neglect. Her left eye resisted closing to the same degree as her right. The muscles that controlled her cheek sagged and her mouth drooped noticeably. Judy's speech was considerably more slurred than only a couple of hours before making any semblance of communication from her almost unintelligible.

As I attempted to sit Judy upright on our couch, she had no core or abdominal stability. Without me applying a consistent pressure against her body, she would topple over. The left side of her body lacked all muscular control or response. It was as if her left side had completely given up and decided that it was done being of any use. In this surreal moment, my brain began to run faster than I knew how to physically respond. *What's going on? How can this be happening again? There is no way this can be happening. We just got home! It's worse than before! What do I do?* These were all questions and statements blazing a path through my mind more rapidly than I could formulate a reply.

Remembering the nurse's exhortation from only a staggering three hours earlier to call him if I encountered any changes in Judy's condition, I laid Judy back down on the couch and quickly dialed his number.

"Hello"

"Hey, this is Eric Foust. I just left the hospital with my wife, Judy, three hours ago and she's not doing well."

"Ok, tell me what's going on?"

"She just woke up from a nap and her condition is worse again. It's like she had another stroke. Her face is drooped, and her speech is slurred."

"Ok, you know that time is critical. I would recommend that you get her back in here immediately. I'll let ED know that you're coming."

"Alright. We're on our way!"

With that, I repeated the same transport process as I had done forty hours earlier. In only a matter of minutes, we were back in the Mercy ED confused, concerned, and contending for Judy in prayer. It was if the roller coaster of emotions had looped around again and I was on board for another unwelcome ride. Feeling a new swell of adrenaline mixed with exhaustion sweep over me, I could sense the angst of the situation traveling through my nervous system. My hands were trembling, my heart was racing, my mind was spinning, and I felt absolutely and completely helpless. For Judy, more MRI's and CT scans filled her evening hours. At one point in the evening while she was off being imaged or scanned, the doctor presented himself and stated that his early examination and assessment were that Judy had possibly suffered more right sided watershed infarcts or even possibly an ICH (intracerebral brain hemorrhage) but that he wouldn't know for sure until the test results returned. Based on that bit of news, it was no surprise when he further informed me that they would be keeping Judy overnight. He had consulted with Dr. Helseth again and determined that she needed to stay in the ED for more observation and a possible new course of action.

Once Judy returned to her ED room, it tore at my heart to even consider leaving her alone in the emergency department for another night. While there was nothing I could do for Judy in this moment other than simply being present, it seemed almost heartless to walk out the door and leave. She seemed so helpless and vulnerable. Yet, I knew she was in good hands. Judy, sensing my internal heart struggle and hesitation, encouraged me through a diminished voice, that it was ok to go. I assured her that I would be back the next day as soon as I was able. With Judy essentially settled for the night and with my responsibilities looming large the next day at church, I kissed her good night and once again headed home to another fitful night of sleep.

The following day was Sunday, September 5, and with it being Labor Day Weekend, most of the primary leadership team from our church were away for the holiday and I was scheduled to preach. Having been kept up to date on Judy's condition, the Lead Team checked in with and questioned me regarding my ability and availability to preach at our two Sunday gatherings given the circumstances. I reassured them that I was ready to go and confident that I would make it through. Even though I'd been writing and delivering sermons on a regular basis for almost 30 years, the weightiness of the responsibility in preaching was never lost on me. It was a sacred task to stand in the midst of a congregation and walk them through a portion of the Bible and, in the process, encounter the God of the Bible. There's a powerful convergence that occurs when the specific word that's been formed in you as a preacher through prepara-tion and study is met with the presence of God and the receptive hearts of people who desperately want to hear what God has to say to them in that moment. When that convergence happens, there is the pivotal opportunity for life change. In an age of chal-lenging opinions and rampant distrust, revealing the heart of God for people and the storyline of redemption and love woven throughout each page of the Bible is so necessary and critical. So for me, engaging in the work of preaching was a joyous and intentional responsibility.

By the power of the Holy Spirit at work in me, I not only preached at both gatherings but felt more empowered and anointed to do so than I had rarely experienced before. God truly met me in my weakness. I recall applying God's gracious and encouraging words to the Apostle Paul for myself as I stepped up to the lectern to speak, "My grace is sufficient for you, for my power is made perfect in weakness" (2 Corinthians 12:9 NIV). I truly encountered His power in my weakness. I am so grateful for the community of "family" that comprised that church. It was a privilege to be a part of who they were and journey through life with them in seasons of joy and trial; victories and failures; hopes and messes. With my responsibilities concluded for the day, I stepped off the stage, weaved my way through the throng of people as the gathering was concluding and quickly exited the building to the isolation of my car. There, in the silence of that 4-door confined space, I exhaled a deep sigh of relief and a pouring out of my emotions followed. Tears of joy over the accomplished work, tears of faithful hope that God was with Judy and I in her distress, and tears of trauma over the unbelievable life circumstances we found ourselves in co-mingled and flowed as one steady stream down my face.

However, needing to revisit Judy as soon as possible, I gathered my composure as best I could and drove back to the hospital. I knew she was counting on me to step into her room at any moment and I desperately wanted to see her face again. As I walked the short distance from the ED entrance to her room, I could feel the tension tightening and the tug of war between hope and despair intensifying in my heart. So much of life is unfortunately like this. I longingly hoped for an overnight miracle where I would enter her room and find Judy, the *normal* Judy, just as she used to be. No drooping facial features. No slurred speech. No muscular issues. No residual stroke symptoms at all. Fully healed! That was my hope. I wasn't being naïve or spiritually ridiculous or clinging to an absurd, impossible wish. I believed that God, in an instant, could extend His hand and heal. I believed that the God who is the same yesterday, today, and forever could still do what He's done in the past. The

degree of our situation was not beyond His capacity to inter-
vene. Why not now? Why not here?

At the same time, despair was wrestling for top billing. But
what if…? What if nothing's changed? What if there's been no
improvement and this is the condition that she'll be harnessed
with from this point forward? What if I don't get my wife back?
Those were dark, transient thoughts that stung my heart and
mind with each step.

Upon arriving in Judy's room, I was met by Drs. Quang and
Helseth. After hurried and seemingly obligatory greetings and
introductions, Dr. Quang stated with precise frankness that
while Judy had improved slightly overnight under ED care, she
did look incrementally worse than she did prior to discharge the
previous day. Not the news or update I was hoping to hear. Also,
while a repeat CT scan revealed no new intracranial hemorrhage
(ICH) and no new infarcts, prior hypodensities were again seen
in the right hemisphere of her brain. After asking for layperson
clarity, Dr. Quang watered down her language to say that while
no indication of bleeding in the brain had appeared, the CT
scan confirmed prior well-defined dense areas in Judy's brain in
comparison to the surrounding tissue and that the darker, dense
areas were the result of possible lack of blood supply to that
portion of the brain. Continuing to inform me of Judy's current
medical status, she said that a computed tomography angiography (CTA) fully confirmed that Judy's right carotid artery was
completely occluded and that her left carotid artery was substan-
tially occluded as well. Based on those findings, Dr. Quang
concluded that, having had a lengthy conversation with Drs.
Helseth and Bey, that the plan would be to conduct a diagnostic
angiogram procedure as soon as possible that afternoon where a
contrasting dye would be injected into her artery to see where
the blockages existed. Following that procedure, there was high
probability of angioplasty or stenting in the occluded arteries.

In a state of ongoing disbelief as this unimaginable plot twist
in our lives continued to unfold, I nodded in agreement with

half-digested understanding as to what was about to happen. It seemed so inconceivable that this medical conversation about brain tissue and blood flow, occlusions and angioplasty was pertaining to Judy…my Judy. I took hold of Judy's right hand and held it for my own sense of comfort and to remind her that we were in this together. I was in it with her.

Around 4:00pm, Dr. Helseth arrived in Judy's room and told us that the earlier "high probability" was now the actual plan. In the next few minutes, Judy would be taken to the Neuro Interventional IR and the delicate procedure of angioplasty or stenting would take place on hopefully both carotid arteries. After finishing detailing the plan and making sure that Judy understood as much as she was able regarding what was about to occur, Dr. Helseth invited me to step outside the room for a conversation beyond the range of Judy's immediate hearing. Once outside earshot, Dr. Helseth placed his hand on my shoulder and explained that while the procedure being performed was common and, in many ways, routine, it did not come without the possibilities of complications, some severe. With optimism combined with reality he said, "I'm expecting everything to go extremely well and for Judy to come through just fine. But anytime you're dealing with major arteries, you have to be prepared for the possibility of things to go wrong in a hurry. If such a situation should arise, we'll do everything in our ability to rectify the situation and stabilize her condition as quickly as possible. Once the procedure is completed, I'll come find you in the surgery waiting room and give you an update. Any questions?" Having none, not because I was fully satisfied with the information and scenario presented to me but because I was at a loss for words as I silently considered an outcome that rendered Judy in a worse condition than she was now, I thanked him for taking the time to speak with me and that I would be praying for him and Judy and anxiously waiting for his follow-up afterwards.

As Dr. Helseth finished, the surgical orderlies appeared and went to work unplugging Judy from all her electrical machines and computers, readying her for her departure. While they worked, I bent over and whispered into Judy's ear that I loved her and that she was fully in God's hands which was the safest place to be. I reminded her that she was the best part of my life. My strength. My joy and that the decision I had made 37 years earlier to join in married life with her was still the best decision I had ever made. With that, I kissed her not knowing if that would be the last kiss we would share. She was now ready to roll and so she gripped my hand and said with a rasp in her voice, "I love you more."

I trekked my way through the hallway maze, following the verbalized directions provided to me, to the OR waiting room. While I had walked many a step with Judy, hand in hand, or with Judy on my mind prior to this short excursion, none carried this level of agonizing seriousness. Judy loved casual jaunts in walking parks or easily traversing a trail in the woods. Even though she wasn't an expert plantsman or gardener, she loved to point out various flowers or foliage that randomly caught her attention. The ones that she could identify by name, she did so with enthusiastic expression. Given my even less than knowledge of the plant world, I would simply smile and enjoy her wonderment. Walking with Judy was always an opportunity to see the vibrancy of her life on full display. People, pets, plants, and panoramic views were all fair game for her curiosity and interest. Not a single person that crossed our paths wasn't greeted without a "good morning" or "good afternoon" or "how are you?" Again, what was in range of vision for Judy mattered to her.

We had walked similar hospital hallways together under painful circumstances and in moments of anguish as we grieved the passing of my parents and her dad. There is something compass shifting that happens within you when the realization that those who raised you and were such prominent influences in your life are no longer physically present. While the death of a parent is expected at some point in time, it's still jarring when it occurs.

Judy and I had also strolled through family birth centers and maternity departments in grief after our own heart-wrenching miscarriage on Mother's Day but more joyfully in celebration of new life being welcomed into the lives of friends and family. We, ourselves, had been ushered along hospital corridors with our own precious gifts of life wrapped tightly in our arms as we joyfully and trepidatiously entered the world of parenting.

Each of our three kids came into this world through their own unique experience. Erika was born at Park Nicollet Methodist Hospital in St. Louis Park, MN on March 10, 1990. Being our first, Judy and I planned and prepared extensively for the arrival of our little girl. From birthing classes to prenatal checkups and examines to pre-Google map days rehearsing our quickest and least obstructive routes from home to hospital, to having all necessary baby items on hand at any given moment, we did it all. We were ready. After a couple of adrenaline-exerting false labor runs, Erika was born naturally and smoothly without any complications. We were parents!

Joel came into our lives on May 21, 1992, at Marshfield Medical Center in Rice Lake, WI. Having left the gender reveal to the actual birth, Judy and I were surprised and elated that our second child was a boy. Joel, however, decided to make his entrance slightly more complicated and tension filled. When Judy went into labor, we naively expected a repeat birthing experience similar to Erika's. Easy (from my perspective), relatively few hours, and natural. But as labor languished into hours without much progression, it became apparent that Joel was in distress. Upon checking the delivery status, the obstetrician noticed that Joel was breech. In addition to that, every time a contraction happened, Joel's heart rate would plummet. A quick ultrasound check indicated that the umbilical cord was being pinched between Joel's head and shoulder necessitating some immediate decisions. While not what Judy and I were hoping for, the decision was made for Judy to undergo a cesarean section. Once the decision was made, Judy was quickly rushed to an operating room while I was equally rushed or, more accurately, thrust into the doctor's breakroom and handed some medical scrubs to put on from head to toe. Which, given the hurried tension of the moment, were surprisingly more difficult to get on correctly than they should have been. As I was escorted into the birthing operating room, Judy was lying on the table already prepped and ready for her c-section. The nurse gave me the option to either stand and watch the c-section unfold and Joel's delivery or I could sit with my attention on Judy's face and be a source of encouragement to her. Given my propensity to faint at the sight of blood or the thought of medical procedures, I chose to be a seated encourager. In the hands of skillful surgeons, Joel was successfully and healthily delivered. We were now the parents of two.

Our third child, Seth, was born on September 6, 1995, at the same hospital as Joel and like Joel, was also breech. He was butt first and unwilling to be persuaded to be otherwise. Given that Judy had already endured a prior c-section, it was communicated to us that it was probably inevitable that Seth would require a c-section as well. But the obstetrician, being an optimist, suggested that he manually try and flip Seth around by pressing on Judy's pregnant belly to see if he could position him in a way that would allow for a normal delivery. On the count of three, the doctor pressed and Seth flipped from butt-first to head down. Success! The hope was that Seth would stay in that position given that his due date was only days away and that he would enter the world through the birth canal designed by God. That hoped quickly vanished as a day before Seth was born, he, under his own determination, squirmed and flipped again butt-first. So the "probably inevitable" became the absolute inevitable and Seth was delivered via c-section and now Judy and I were outnumbered by children…3 to 2. Our family was now complete as we were blessed with three healthy, beautiful children.

Now, a lifetime later, I found myself in a lifeless, cold OR waiting room. Due to COVID-19 restrictions firmly and uncompromisingly in strict adherence at the hospital, no visitors, guests, or members of my support team were allowed to join me in the waiting. Instead, I sat alone with a solitary window to the outside world. As the late summer sun began to set, I watched as time moved in concert with the shadows across the room highlighting the antiseptically sterile floor. The pastel green faux leather furniture captured the shadow of the window frame as the sun continued its movement. The sole companionship of the setting sun only magnified the silence and quietness of the space. All the external voices were gone. No more instructions, directions, or medical explanations were being audibly communicated. I was left with only my own internal voices which were deeply loud. It is amazing how when the endless deafening and intrusive sounds of the world around us are shut out, that the internal dialogue rushes to fill the newfound void often with the same intrusiveness. My private conversations covered the spectrum of all the "what ifs," the potential complications, what life could look like for us, let alone for Judy, if the surgery didn't go according to plan, to interspersed self-reminders of hope that God was fully in control and that He was my, and Judy's, anchor of peace. I found momentary comfort in these words, "I am leaving you with a gift—peace of mind and heart. And the peace I give is a gift the world cannot give. So don't be troubled or afraid" (John 14:27 NLT).

After a several hours of solitude, my phone rang breaking the silence. On the other end was Dr. Helseth.

"Eric, Dr. Helseth here. The surgery was actually rougher than we anticipated but Judy came through and we're wrapping everything up at the moment. She'll be moved shortly to post op recovery where she'll be for a while but then you can come and see her. In the meantime, just hang tight and we'll come get you. I can provide you with more details in a little bit."

I thanked him and ended the call, relieved and yet anxious over what world I would be walking into with Judy post-surgery. Approximately thirty minutes later, the OR waiting room door slowly opened and a member of the hospital staff, fully clothed in medical scrubs, sheepishly peered in and calmly, with a hushed tone in his voice as if he was disturbing me, asked if I was Eric.

I enthusiastically responded that I was, hoping for an invitation to join Judy.

At my response, the medical team member approached me and, violating hospital COVID protocol, sat down next to me and put his hand on my shoulder, which in the moment, seemed like an unwelcome invasion of my personal space in my prior cloistered confines. With his hand firmly on my shoulder he said solemnly, "I am so sorry for your loss."

"Wait! What?!" I exclaimed in shock.

"I just want to express my condolences for the loss of your wife," he proceeded to share.

Abruptly interrupting him, I emphatically stated, "No, my wife just came out of surgery! The surgeon just called me and said that she came through fine. You've got the wrong wife!"

Confused and bewildered, the medical staff member asked, "But your name is Eric, correct?"

"Yes, it is," I responded again.

"And your wife is Gwen, correct?" he hesitatingly queried.

"No, I'm Eric but my wife is Judy," I quickly corrected him.

In that moment, all the color vanished from his face and he embarrassingly and apologetically said, "I am so sorry. I've got the wrong Eric. I must have misunderstood the message given to me. It's been a long, tough day."

At that, he got up to exit the room leaving me with an accelerated heart rate and mental whiplash. But as he reached the door, I asked, as if the words were leaving my mouth without my control, if he had any further update on my wife. Barely turning his head in my direction, he unemotionally replied, "No, but I'm sure she's fine." Which, given his prior medical misinformation, didn't come across as very reassuring.

With the door closing behind him, I was once again left in my solitude to contemplate the craziness of the conversation that had just been exchanged. As the quietness and calmness resettled, that brief invasion of confusion, misinformation, an unhelpful voice, unintentional but hurtful words, and uninvited stress-induced panic was a microcosm of what we can often experience numerous times throughout our day. Each of those microcosmic intrusions, if given the power and space, can radically morph into a macrocosmic disruption or, more tragically, can alter and shake the perception of our reality, our identity, our faith, and halt or inaccurately redirect the momentum of our lives. Intrusive moments such as this or more frequently, intrusive thoughts that mentally grip us throughout the day are frantic and fear-inducing. They, almost always, are rooted in the worst conclusion or outcome possible and yell into our lives with ferocity. They make our palms sweat, our heart race, and our blood pressure rise. They keep us up at night and cause our minds to run in a myriad of hectic and spiraling directions. These intrusions in our day or thought process betray our understanding of reality.

In light of this very present occurrence the Apostle Paul wrote these words of exhortation, "We demolish arguments and every pretension that sets itself up against the knowledge of God, and we take captive every thought to make it obedient to Christ" (2 Corinthians 10:5 NLT). The original audience of Paul's instruction were a group of Christ-followers in the city of Corinth who were being influenced away from their foundation of belief with lies contrary to the truth of God's Word. He was encouraging them to actively and aggressively reign in those intrusive moments and thoughts with what they knew to be true. We…I…need to do the same. When intrusions are allowed to run rampant, they can do untold damage. Our counter offensive needs to be to breathe, remember and reclaim what we know to be true, and shut down the internal dialogue that has reared its ugly head. Thankfully, I had a few moments in the waiting to compose my thoughts, catch my breath, and reorient myself to my present reality that Judy was alive and recovering from surgery. Life, at least for this instant, was stable.

Another two hours had passed when a nurse entered my waiting room and asked me to follow her to ICU where Judy was resting and recovering. Leaving the waiting room, I followed my guide through more corridors lined with room after room of patients in various degrees of distress, alarms alerting nurses to immediate needs, and staff checking medications and charting their activities on mobile workstations. While there was a level of organized chaos to the scene, it all elevated my own emotions of anticipation and fear of what I would be walking into. Arriving at the ICU, we were met with imposing large metal doors unable to be opened without proper authorization. Having scanned her credentials, the doors slowly swung open in response to the nurse's permission to enter, ushering me into a new, inner sanctum comprised of beeps and alarms that were seemingly more significant and serious than previous similar sounds.

The ICU was designed in a semi-circle with a limited number of rooms around the perimeter and the nurses' station as the central hub. Medical personnel appeared to rush from room to room with a greater degree of immediacy. Conversations were more hushed. The atmosphere seemed more somber, more vigilant, more hyper focused, more critical. Trying not to look or cross the invisible threshold between public and private space, each room I passed contained an individual whose body was fighting for survival as family members stood or sat with helpless attention. Some weeping, some making necessary phone calls, and others carrying on one-sided conversations with their non-communicative loved ones. Judy was given a private room with a floor to ceiling glass window and a sliding glass door allowing her to be fully visible to the nurses' station. A thin blue curtain could be pulled to shield her from inadvertent glances when more privacy was needed.

I stopped briefly outside the entrance to her room long enough to check my composure level and take a deep breath. Stepping into Judy's world, I found her sleeping which eased my anxiety. For the most part, she looked the same as before. I guess I'm not exactly sure what condition I expected to find Judy in, but I was definitely expecting worse than what I saw in this moment. A blood pressure cuff, multiple wrist bands with scan codes, and a finger pulse oximeter lined her right arm. Wires attached to numerous sensors strategically placed on her skin were exiting her hospital gown, all connected to monitors recording important data. A nasogastric tube had been inserted through her nose and into her stomach to deliver nutrition and medication to her body in the absence of being able to physically swallow. Not wanting to wake her but desperately wanting to hold her hand and feel the reassuring warmth of her skin, I searched beneath the blankets until I was able to secure her left hand in mine. It was non-responsive but warm. It communicated life. I gently rubbed my thumb over her thumb which was entirely for my comfort, not hers.

Dr. Helseth entered Judy's room and proceeded to give me a recount of her surgery. Attempts to open the right internal carotid artery occlusion were unsuccessful. After a few unsuccessful tries with a microwire and microcatheter system and time starting to work against him, he switched to the left internal carotid artery where successful angioplasty and stenting were performed. In describing the procedure, he outlined how he had inserted a thin, flexible catheter in her groin and threaded it up to the occluded area in her neck. The catheter has a tiny, deflated balloon at the tip. When the balloon reached the blocked portion of her carotid artery, the balloon was inflated, opening the artery. Immediately following the opening of the artery, a tiny mesh stent was put into place between the distal common carotid artery and in the internal carotid artery with the intent of keeping that artery open. He further explained that a primary reason it had taken longer than expected to move Judy from surgery to recovery was that upon being transferred to the ICU, Judy was found to be unresponsive with posturing and a right gaze deviation. Once again being lost in the medical terminology, he simplified his language for me to say that upon arrival, she was unresponsive and that her body was evidencing a level of "posturing" where her arms were bent and rigidly held near the middle of her chest. Her fists were clenched, and her legs were straight with her feet pointing outwards. Given the seriousness of this situation, Judy was emergently rushed back for a CT scan to either reveal or rule out an intracranial hemorrhage and for a repeat angiography which revealed small blood clotting within the stent. The decision was made, at the time, not to perform any more interventions but for her to be placed on a dopamine infusion and Integrilin to maintain a more regular blood pressure and help lessen and eradicate the presence of blood clots.

The following days were clear and traumatic indicators that we were in the deep end of the pool regarding Judy's condition. By September 7, her condition had significantly regressed. The stroke and its complications had resulted in total left side neglect. She had zero ability to move or feel anything on the left side of her body, was more lethargic, and was evidencing cognitive slowing. Judy's right gaze deviation was heart wrenchingly apparent as she was unable to look to the left past the midline of her face. My Judy was alive and present but not the same. She had always been my true north, my home, my source of stability, my counterbalance to life. Yet the Judy in front of me was unable to demonstrate any of those qualities. The vibrant, interactive, extroverted, independent woman I had come to know and love was now seemingly trapped in her own body, unable to break free. Several more CT scans and MRI's confirmed that Judy had suffered multiple right hemisphere ischemic cerebral infarcts combined with right carotid territory watershed strokes. Judy's medical notes revealed the growing list of concerns...

Left visual field loss.

Dense left hypodensities in her cerebral white matter.

Dense sensory loss on left side.

Dysarthria (slurred speech).

Left facial weakness and numbness.

Left lower facial droop

Left side neglect.

Left upper extremity with no motor function visible whatsoever.

Left lower extremity no response to command.

With Judy's condition in the critical stage, our three kids and their spouses decided it was necessary to fly from their various destinations to Redding to be with their mom. As they arrived, we found ourselves in the holding pattern of uncertainty, not knowing if her condition would continue to regress or rebound and they wanted to be present. Unable to calculate what the future would hold was excruciatingly immobilizing. Again, with the COVID protocols, only one of us was allowed to be in her ICU room at a time. So, like the passing of the baton in a relay race, one of us would sign out, the next would sign in and we'd take our staggered individual allotment of time with her. But no matter who was in the room, all we could do was watch and wait.

The trauma and agony held within the framework of the ICU was a continual dispiriting reminder that life can be interrupted with cruel and uncaring harshness. The room adjacent to Judy's was occupied by a young man who was on his fourth week in the ICU due to injuries suffered in a severe car accident. Due to his anxiety and anger over the current situation of his life, he would thrash in his bed in an attempt to get up resulting in an onslaught of alarms being set off. Nurses would rush in, and a present family member would work to console him, offer reassurance, and remind him of the medical and life saving necessity of remaining calm. This consoling work would bring a temporary reprieve to his agitation but within moments, the scene would be repeated again.

In a room within eyesight and earshot to Judy's was a wife holding a bedside vigil for her husband who was, by evidence of the emotions being expressed and the muted lighting, in the final stages of life. The wife's grieving over her impending loss could not be contained within the confines of her heartbreaking space. Every once in a while, her phone would ring and she would step out of the room and give a hushed update through her tears. Once her call was completed, she would step back into her current reality and resume her stance by his bed.

As agonizing as those scenes were to be privy to, our obvious primary concern and attention was fixated on Judy. Being slightly more awake for short segments of time, she tried to converse but with the feeding tube down her throat and slurred speech it was a difficult ordeal for both her and us. At one point in a moment of being awake, I was able to decipher that she was thirsty and wanted a drink. What she requested caught me slightly off guard. "I want an apple juice on the rocks." Thinking I misunderstood, I asked her to repeat what she said. With the same emphatic desire she said, "I want an apple juice on the rocks." Now Judy is not even a casual drinker so for her to ask for anything on the rocks was extremely humorous and so "Judy-like." Her humor once again being evidenced even in trying circumstances and life teetering in the balance.

This entire isolated, insulated, and trauma infused subculture contained within the ICU was such a contrast to the world beyond the restricted entry of the metal doors. Society beyond is conformed, pressured, and pressed to run at such a frenetic pace to its own self detriment. We always need to be "on the go," accomplishing more, working harder, working longer, achieving greater accomplishments, overstretching ourselves to meet higher expectations, ignoring the flashing red lights of burnout, all at the expense of personal health, relational connection, and family priorities. We are conditioned to suppress our weaknesses and self-promote our strengths. So much so that we very rarely settle in stillness long enough to look up and see life unfolding directly in front of us. But within the ICU, everything outside is forced, to a great degree, to come to a halt. You are forced to see, to hear, to feel what is clearly in your immediate range of sight. Personal self-accomplishments and self-striving are abruptly rendered secondary to the primary needs of another laying before you. We are given the space, albeit under unwelcome circumstances, to feel the heaviness of possible losses and the hope of potential recovery. In essence, we are given a forced "time out" to evaluate.

In those early ICU days, there came a point where a critical test needed to be performed. A swallow test. Judy had been receiving nutrients and medication through her feeding tube but it became crucial for forward momentum in recovery to test her swallowing ability. This test was critical for several reasons. One reason was to evaluate the neurological control of her swallowing reflex. If her swallowing reflex had become impaired as a result of her stroke, then there was the high probability of food going down the wrong tube causing choking and aspiration leading to possible pneumonia. A second reason was in order to gradually move Judy to a more regular diet to improve her health and strength. The swallow test would be administered by Speech Therapists and was a huge hurdle for Judy to clear.

Given Judy's physical impairments and her left side neglect, the decision was made to administer the swallow test at her bedside. When it came time for the swallow evaluation, one concern was Judy's limited alertness. It was extremely difficult for her to stay engaged with any instructions or activity beyond a brief amount of time. Ruth, the Speech Therapist, repositioned Judy upright in her bed at a ninety-degree angle and laid out for Judy and me the instructions and the possible outcomes we could expect. My palms were sweating and my heart was racing with anticipation and hopefulness for Judy as I stood and watched this evaluation begin to unfold. It didn't take long though for me to become an active participant. Ruth proceeded to give Judy a small sip of thin liquid from a spoon but with Judy's waxing and waning attention span and cognitive connection to the present activity, it called for both Ruth and I to strongly verbally and visually encourage and stimulate Judy to stay in the moment.

The first evaluation resulted in Judy choking and coughing as her swallowing reflex failed, allowing the liquid to escape into her trachea. Not only was this traumatic for Judy but it was definitely traumatic for me to witness as she gasped for breath and fought to clear her windpipe. After a brief recovery period in which Judy drifted off to sleep, a second evaluation was attempted. Again, with maximum team participation and repeated cues, Judy was able to produce a minimal amount of swallowing production before another choking ordeal. Once the coughing was cleared, Judy drifted back to sleep again. Needless to say, it was readily apparent that Judy's evaluation did not conclude with a ringing endorsement. With Judy asleep after her brief but strenuous exertion, Ruth sympathetically but factually stated to me that Judy was dealing with what appeared to be moderate to severe pharyngeal dysphagia. She simply wasn't able to engage her swallowing muscles enough to prevent aspiration into her lungs. Having seen the proof with my own eyes, I nodded in disappointed agreement.

Having communicated the reality, Ruth offered a bit of optimism and encouragement. She suggested that a second swallowing test be done the following day except rather than being evaluated in her bed where it was harder for Judy to stay alert and engaged, they do the evaluation in a swallow study chair which would allow for Judy's head to maintain a more upright and neutral position. As disappointed as I was for Judy in the present failure, this suggestion offered a fresh glimmer of hope and moving her in the right direction. I was willing to try anything on Judy's behalf short of causing her additional undue trauma or setback if it meant that we could turn the corner to the recovery onramp.

With the swallow study chair evaluation set for the following day, the room was emptied again of therapy and medical personnel as quickly as they appeared. The present whirlwind was over. Once again, the rhythmic sounds of Judy's machines and monitors filled the space. The steady rhythm was only broken by the occasional obnoxious beeping of the oximeter when Judy's oxygen levels dipped too low. A couple of deeper breaths would reset the oximeter and silence the beeping. As the news of Judy's failed swallow test was reported through the various departments that needed to know, it was finally communicated to me that due to her diminished alertness and high aspiration risk that she would not be a candidate for the ice chip plan. For those who have been in a similar fluid restricted situation, you know how ice chips are almost like heaven sent gifts. Each tiny chip providing an oasis of liquid in a dry mouth desert. This is not an exaggeration.

Along with the denial of the ice chip plan came a strict NPO order. NPO comes from the Latin which means "*nil per os*" and when applied to the medical field it is translated as "nothing by mouth." So, Judy was restricted from ingesting anything by mouth...hydration, nutrition, and medication. Everything she needed would be supplied through her nasogastric feeding tube.

The reality of another possible defeat in the swallowing arena had my stomach in knots as Judy was being positioned in the blue swallow study chair. Like Nehemiah standing before King Ataxerxes and facing a serious situation that carried enormous weight for his people in Nehemiah 2, I quickly and silently prayed to the God of heaven for my person, Judy. Mentally imploring God for even a small victory. Pillows were placed behind her head to help maintain a neutral position. The longer she sat in the study chair the more she would drift and lean to the left and so more support was added to keep her core upper body as upright and centered as possible. Since it was earlier in the morning, however, and in the swallow study chair compared to her bed during the previous day's evaluation, Judy was more alert and aware of the procedure and what was at stake. As the instructions were given, she responded in short phrases and affirmative understanding but still wasn't able to voluntarily follow the commands without repeated tactile cues.

With the situation prepped as much as it was going to be, the speech therapist and the radiology technician asked if Judy was ready. As she looked at me with some trepidation in her eyes, I winked at her and said reassuringly, "You've got this. You're ready." It was all systems go.

A small amount of thin liquid was placed on a spoon and cautiously placed in Judy's mouth. A small swallow was triggered. Never before had the word "triggered" felt so positive.

Next, a limited amount of liquid was administered through a straw. After a short reflexive cough, another swallow was triggered.

Moving up the consistency ladder, a thickened nectar was given to Judy via a spoon again. A swallow was triggered. We were 3 for 3. Judy was batting a thousand.

Now came the most important attempt of all. This would be the one to determine whether or not Judy could possibly transition from the feeding tube to a more substantial diet even if that meant pureed food. It was the "apple sauce" test.

A small spoonful of apple sauce was gently placed in Judy's mouth. I intently watched as the muscles worked to maneuver the apple sauce into position. They instantly constricted, closing off her airway and initiating a swallow. The apple sauce successfully cleared into her esophagus. Never before had I been so thankful and happy about apple sauce.

The speech therapist, the radiologist, and I broke into cheers and applause. Judy had passed this critical juncture in her recovery. As a crooked smile emerged on Judy's face, an overwhelming rush of relief and pride over what she had accomplished flooded my heart. This was the biggest win in the early days of her journey!

Having returned Judy to her ICU room and repositioned her back in her bed, I was given a list of recommendations and strategies regarding Judy's diet moving forward. She would require constant feeding assistance at every meal from either myself or a nurse with an awareness of any food pocketing on the left side of her mouth. She would be placed on a pureed diet along with mildly thickened nectar to drink and all medications could now be crushed and added in her puree.

After each meal, it was suggested that Judy remain upright in bed for at least forty-five minutes to ensure that everything had passed into her stomach without any reflux. It was subsequently decided to leave the nasogastric feeding tube in place until a consistent routine and a tolerance for swallowing and digestion had been established.

At 6:00pm, I heard the rumbling wheels of the metal food cart as it was rolled into the ICU. Shortly after, the ICU nurse appeared at Judy's door with a food tray in hand and carefully placed it on her bedside stand. The tray contained a carton of nectar, a cup of thickened water and a covered plate. Lifting the lid revealed a plate of pureed peas, pureed potatoes with extra gravy, and pureed beef stroganoff. While not necessarily inviting or appealing to the eye, it was a beautiful ensemble of nutrition that resembled food not offered through a tube. In this moment, it was heaven on a plate. Following the earlier detailed instructions presented to me, I spoon fed Judy her first pureed meal with care, concern, and caution. I was so intent on not doing anything that would create a coughing episode, a harmful reaction or cause any alarms or bells to go off due to my carelessness or ineptness.

Judy was an exceptional ICU patient even in her limited capacity. To the best of her ability, she attempted to follow directions given to her, participate in speech therapy, and be an encourager to those who were caring for her. As a child, Judy had always wanted to be a good girl, never a disappointment. I remember her recalling how, from her earliest memories, she worked hard to avoid being in trouble or drawing negative attention to herself. Even though she was a talkative extrovert, she never wanted to be a troublemaker. The last thing she wanted was to draw the ire or anger of her dad or really of anyone in authority. To be disciplined was a crushing blow to her spirit. Now that doesn't mean that Judy wasn't a typical sibling who knew how to press the buttons, especially of her younger sister, Nancy. She knew how to provoke and irritate Nancy to no end and, I believe, Nancy returned the favor with equal enjoyment. But that sibling irritation transformed into deep sibling love over the years and became a precious gift that Judy was extremely grateful and thankful for. Judy, however, was a rule follower through and through. If possible, she stayed within the boundaries of what was safe and right. Not only for her wellbeing but also for the wellbeing and success of others. After encountering a personal faith in Christ, Judy's drive to do what was right was fully born out of her desire to walk in obedience to and as an expression of the love of God. This was her motivation, "If we love God, we will do whatever he tells us to. And he has told us from the very first to love each other" (2 John 1:6 NLT). Judy didn't want to do anything what would intentionally or purposefully diminish her life from being a living, walking example of the command to love others. She wanted everyone to encounter what she had encountered.

I, on the other hand, found that I possessed a before unknown or, at least, an untapped aspect of my personality that was easily riled up, on edge, and quick to lash out in response to any perceived injustice or lack of attention given to Judy. It was an unexpected, strange introduction to what would become a needed character trait of advocacy on Judy's behalf. But the strangeness of this new side to myself was because it was so opposite of my normal, even keeled personality. It takes a lot for me to get worked up and voice my frustration. So much so that it became a consistent joke amongst the team that I previously worked with that they were waiting for the day or the time or the event where I would "lose it" and go off uncorked. They wanted to see an unleashed Eric Foust in comparison to the controlled, even tempered, unflustered me. While I laughed at the joke and their expectant desire to see me fly off the handle in unrestrained chaos, I never wanted to find myself in that position. It was so antithetical to who I was that it frightened me, to a degree, to envision myself being forced to that kind of outburst. Yet, in reaction to Judy's present reality, I was ready to fly off the handle without notice. I'm sure that much of that was due to the internal pain and trauma I was experiencing and was now being turned outward to the unsuspecting medical personnel who were simply attempting to do their jobs.

As the days in ICU continued to add up, making each day almost inseparable and indistinguishable from the one before it, Judy's mind and body fought to regain precious ground that had been lost. In this surreal time and space, I, with tears constantly welling up in my eyes, would watch the therapist work with Judy on the simplest of tasks. On one particular day, the therapist put a toothbrush in Judy's affected left hand and cupped her fingers around the toothbrush handle. Given Judy's inability to grip the toothbrush herself, the therapist assisted in helping keep the handle in place and lifted it towards Judy's mouth. Reflexively, Judy raised her *right* hand to her mouth, touching her lips in search of the toothbrush. On account of her left side visual loss, she was unable to see where the toothbrush was actually located. The therapist inquisitively asked, "What are you doing?" Judy replied, "I'm looking for the toothbrush." With the toothbrush in, what should have been, easy line of sight, the therapist asked, "where's it at?" Watching this unfold and unable to hold back, I jumped in and interjected my encouragement for Judy to look to her left. Immediately I felt like an overzealous participant having just given away the secret answer to the exam. But having done so, she replied to the therapist's question, "It's right in front of me." This snapshot of Judy's early therapy was one of many moments when after such interactions I needed to step outside the confines of her ICU room and allow the emotions to flow. It was gut-wrenching.

Judy spent two weeks in ICU before being transferred to "the floor." "The floor" was simply the code language for being moved from ICU to a "regular" room on the first floor. While on the surface this transfer could seem like a graduation as a result of Judy's physical improvement, it was rather a lateral move to open ICU bedspace as Judy's condition had only slightly progressed. The primary progression was that Judy's diet had escalated from pureed to minced. On the scorecard of her overall needed recovery, this was a minimal gain but still a gain.

While in Room 100 on "the floor," Judy had two phenomenal nurses both named Ashley which helped me tremendously with name recognition. Both Ashleys went above and beyond with their attention to and care of Judy. The damn stroke had rendered Judy incontinent. A humbling and traumatizing casualty of losing so much bodily function. Not only was she unable to control her urinary and bowel functions but she was unable to tell when or if she had gone. This present reality was so embarrassing to Judy and the awareness of her inability to do anything about it reduced her to tears so often. She hated this most of all. Encountering Judy's grief, the Ashleys were compassionately militant in making sure that Judy was clean, dry, and infection free in order to maintain healthy hygiene and skin care. As if consoling herself or, in her mind, easing the burden of being cleaned and changed, Judy would turn her face towards me and with tears running down her cheeks, softly say, "I'm sorry." It broke my heart every time. Gratefully, the Ashleys constantly reassured her that it was ok even if Judy didn't feel like it was. They were on her team.

It was under their watch that Judy received her first hair washing with real water, shampoo, and drying since she entered the hospital. I had fumbled through a couple of dry shampoo attempts while Judy was in ICU, but the outcome only confirmed my lack of salon expertise. Her hair appeared cleaner, combed and more orderly than prior to my attempts but far from anything stylish. But the more noticeable failure was that the aerosol spray from the dry shampoo canister left a wafting haze in the room similar to the smog hovering over Los Angeles on a hot summer day. I half expected the lingering odor to either set off the smoke alarms or Judy's oxygen sensor or both.

The wonder of Ashley's personal care of Judy is that it offered a small respite of normalcy. It wasn't a massive medical procedure which she performed successfully. It wasn't a monumental breakthrough in physical or speech therapy that launched Judy forward in her recovery. Ashley simply washed her hair. She demonstrated concern and attention and personal worth to Judy by the kindest and simplest of actions. In the moment, it was a gamechanger. And as a result, Judy's demeanor beamed with fresh beauty. She felt more alive than she'd felt in weeks. This one action had a direct connection to Judy's heart. What a powerful reminder that the smallest actions, which may seem inconsequential in the moment, can have deep and significant impact. Too often what's recognized and deemed worthy of attention are the extremely magnanimous acts of philanthropy and charity and there's certainly nothing wrong with those outward expression towards others. But in a society of comparison, those actions can diminish the value of the simple and small but no less noteworthy. For me, Ashley was demonstrating, through an intentional act of kindness, Jesus' words when asked by the religious establishment what the most important commandment was, "And you must love the Lord your God with all your heart, all your soul, all your mind, and all your strength. The second command is equally important: ***Love your neighbor as yourself*** (Mark 12:30 NLT). Ashley loved her neighbor...patient...as herself and Judy felt seen and valued.

As the hospital stay lingered on, the restrictions enforced by COVID-19 wore on both Judy and me. The inability for her to receive visitors and my long days of bedside vigil alone created a tangible separation from our internal world and the world outside the confines of the hospital. But even though that was our daily existence, I'm so grateful for the numerous expressions of love and support that came our way. As I stayed current with our family and friends through social media, powerful posts, responses, and words of encouragement hit my feed and I gladly shared them with Judy. Prophetic dreams and prayers of hope, healing, and recovery were shared with us, reinvigorating my resolve to stay present and re-energizing Judy to stay in the fight…

"Hang in there to both of you. God, and you, Eric, are closing the exit door because it's not time for Judy to exit. Ephesians 3: 14-21 are my life verses and I will be praying them over you. 'Heavenly Father, thank you for purchasing Judy. Thank you she is of precious value to you. Thank you for her redemption. Jesus, thank you for the stripes you took for her. Thank you that by those stripes, healing is hers. Thank you for working out this salvation. You love her and have established her. You have fixed her boundaries. Let those boundaries fall in pleasant places. Let Judy and Eric praise your name forever. Give them the gifts of patience and persistence as they move forward. Close their ears to any lies of the enemy of their souls. We ask You for complete healing and restoration for Judy in the name of the Lord Jesus Christ.'"

"Heavenly Father, thank you for purchasing Judy. Thank you that she is of precious value to you. Thank you for her redemption. Jesus, thank you for the stripes you took for her. Thank you that by those stripes, healing is hers. Thank you for working out this salvation. You love her and have established her. You have fixed her boundaries. Let those boundaries fall in pleasant places. Let Judy and Eric praise your name forever. Give them the gifts of patience and persistence as they move forward. Close their ears to any lies of the enemy of their souls. We ask You for complete healing and restoration for Judy in the name of the Lord Jesus Christ."

Much needed and timely phone calls from dear, long-time

friends at all hours of the day and night provided a salve to my heart. One evening a group of friends gathered outside the entrance of the hospital and with outstretched arms in the direction of Judy's room, they prayed and interceded before the throne of God on her behalf.

I took those prayers and words of encouragement as heavenly equilibrium to balance my emotional roller coaster. The juxtaposition of the reality of physical infirmity and the need for physical healing was working overtime in me. I wanted so deeply to carry enough faith for both Judy and I to *make* healing happen. Even though my theology of healing had been adjusted, I found myself falling back into the mindset of my youth that if prayed *hard enough,* if I said *enough right* words, if I prayed with *enough sincerity*, God would be *obligated* to heal. The spiritual equation of my striving and doing it right plus my effort to do enough would guarantee the results I was expecting. God would magically be happy with me and acquiesce to my needs…or in this case, Judy's needs. As if my words could twist God's arm on my behalf. How similar were my efforts to Jesus' instruction when he was teaching the disciples how to pray, "When you pray, don't babble on and on as the Gentiles do. They think their prayers are answered merely by repeating their words again and again" (Matthew 6:5 NLT). Thankfully God's love and mercy covers our manipulative agendas and our faulty notions, at times, of what we think is best. But the reality was that even if my prayers were theologically "ify," the intent and request were absolutely genuine…Judy's miraculous healing. I wanted my Judy back. I wanted my wife and the mother of our kids and grandmother to our grandchildren back the way she was before. But what if that wasn't the story that God was writing for her and us?

The hospital social services representative appeared in the doorway of Judy's room asking to meet with me. We were now on Day 23 of Judy's hospitalization. The time had come to consider the next steps for her as she couldn't stay in the hospital indefinitely. Every new corner we turned was a step into foreign and unchartered territory for me. Having no previous experience or wisdom to fall back on and help navigate the decisions needed to be made, everything felt vulnerable, overwhelming, and a matter of life and death. Every decision carried a plethora of second guesses and "what ifs."

The social services rep calmly and compassionately introduced me to the necessary next step of rehab and transitioning Judy to an in-patient rehabilitation facility. As the words were being spoken so effortlessly by her, each statement was hammering me with the unrelenting surrealness of our circumstances. Long term Rehabilitation. Intense therapy. Hopeful but no guarantee of recovery. Limited facility options. Ongoing COVID restrictions. Physically unable to continue treatment at the hospital. Insurance hurdles. It all kept adding up as an insurmountable mountain.

"What are our facility options?" I asked with hesitancy and trepidation. Knowing that Judy's insurance coverage at the time was less than widely accepted, I expected the answer to be less than ideal but I resolved to remain optimistic. The social services rep replied, "I'll give it to you straight. We don't have much to work with."

My heart sank as my optimism plummeted and I'm sure it clearly registered in my expression.

"But it's not hopeless," she continued. "Given COVID capacity restrictions at most facilities, the unacceptance of Judy's insurance, and the level of therapy that Judy requires, we only have two options. One is local and the other is in Sacramento."

I was tired of difficult decisions, lack of clear direction, and the uncertainty of choosing what was best. I wanted somebody to simply and unmistakably explain to me the one clear, best decision that would solve my dilemmas and speed Judy to recovery. Decision-making exhaustion, brain fog, trauma overload, and the ongoing interruption of any normal daily rhythm was taking its toll on me and my ability to process information.

I blurted out as I sought a decision-making reprieve, "If it was your spouse, which would you choose?"

"The local one is a fine facility. It's obviously in town which makes it convenient for you. While it has everything needed to help facilitate Judy's therapy, it doesn't have the best reviews. They are currently understaffed and so the residents may not receive the most attentive personal care."

"The facility in Sacramento is a highly respected facility that primarily focuses on neurorestorative therapy which is exactly what Judy needs. She would receive physical, speech, and occupational therapy every day. The downside is that this facility is three hours away from where you currently live."

"If it was my spouse and my decision," she continued, "I'd choose the facility in Sacramento for quality and level of care."

Committed and determined to provide Judy with the best that I could possibly give her, I chose NeuroRestorative-Granite Bay (Sacramento).

PART II

Granite Bay

I had wept countless tears over the month of Judy's hospitalization at Mercy but I was not prepared for the onslaught of emotion that would overwhelm me on the morning of her transfer to NeuroRestorative-Granite Bay. Both Judy and I had grown to love her nursing team at Mercy. Their care, attention, and protection of Judy had done much to provide comfort and compassion on the darkest and most trying early days and nights of her stroke recovery. With each press of the call button, they responded with urgency and concern, no matter how small or menial the request might have been. We got to know them, not as nursing staff, but as friends. In an unbelievable nightmare, our hearts had melded with theirs. The rotation of nurses may have simply been doing their job but for Judy and I, they were life-givers.

The transfer and transition of Judy to her NeuroRestorative destination carried significant challenges. For starters, as I already mentioned, NeuroRestorative-Granite Bay was located three hours away from where we lived and from where Judy was currently hospitalized. The transfer required her to travel that distance via medical transport. Three hours on a gurney in the back of an ambulance. Also, given the geographical distance from home and my need to maintain a semblance of work in order to keep up with the compassionless demand to pay bills, my visitation abilities would be radically altered. Meaning that I wouldn't be able to see her every day. Meaning there would be days when Judy would be alone. I could barely comprehend that reality. On top of that, Judy's in-patient rehabilitation would last, at a minimum, from 10-12 weeks. But those tangible challenges all paled in comparison to the mental and emotional anguish that Judy would experience being disconnected from community, being thrust into a new, unknown environment, forced to face her deficits, at times, alone, and awakening more and more to the possibility of a disabled future with an impaired brain.

Social Services and nurses informed us that the transport team would be arriving around 11:00am. That announcement provided time for Judy to finish her minced breakfast and for me to pack the minimal personal belongings that she had with her. Due to COVID, I was given permission to practically take anything with me that wasn't furniture or medical equipment as it would all be thrown away after Judy's release. So in the free-for-all, I grabbed the back wedges, all the extra incontinence briefs, unused chux pads, creams, lotions, and anything else that I thought would be of benefit to her down the road. I filled two bags worth of precious commodities. Feeling more like a burglar trying to inconspicuously escape with valuable loot in broad daylight, I weaved my way out of the hospital and to the car with my bagged booty, avoiding eye contact along the way until I was able to unload it all in the privacy of my vehicle.

Returning to Judy's room, the station nurse and the doctor on the floor presented me with the discharge orders.

As the clock slowly inched its way towards 11:00, I could see and feel the anxiety and tension growing in Judy. She nervously asked every few minutes if it was 11:00 yet. She was distressed about how the transfer from the bed to the gurney was going to take place, how she was going to make the trip to Sacramento, whether I was going to make the trip with her, and would she be ok. I calmly attempted to reassure her that everything was going to be fine and that, more importantly, she was going to be fine. With every question or concern, tears welled up in her eyes and she reached out for a comforting hold of her hand. I leaned in and softly sang to her the lullaby that we sang to our young children every night to end their day with peace as they were falling asleep. As my voice choked with emotion, I reminded her, "the Lord make his face shine on you and be gracious to you; the Lord turn his face toward you and give you peace" (Numbers 6:25-26 NIV).

The increased level of conversation and the sound of maneuvering the transport gurney in the hallway indicated that the time for Judy's discharge and departure had arrived. With the square footage in Judy's room at a premium, I stepped into the hallway to give extra space for the nurses and transport team to do their thing. Having aligned the gurney parallel with the bed and having carefully placed the portable transport sling under her body, the two nurses and the two team members each firmly took hold of a grab handle and on the count of three, with routine experience, lifted Judy from the hospital bed and over to the gurney.

The transport team proceeded to strap Judy securely to the bed, tilted the gurney to an upright position, placed a pillow behind her head, and covered her with a blanket. Within minutes, like a well-oiled NASCAR pit crew, they had Judy physically, if not mentally or emotionally, set for a road trip. It was "go" time.

Leaving what had become our temporary "second home," the team wheeled Judy past the nurses' station and paused for them to each give her a hug and say goodbye. The tears flowed from everyone who wished Judy the best in the next phase of her recovery. Her impact on the staff was clearly evident and I was filled with appreciation and love for Judy's ability to connect so deeply, so effortlessly.

As I followed the transport procession through the hospital corridors, I held my emotions in check but they were ready to explode when given freedom. Once outside, Judy's gurney was turned and positioned with her back to the ambulance rear doors. This was her first re-exposure to sun and fresh air in over a month. But it was anything but refreshing for Judy. She was grieving deeply. Fear, uncertainty, change, and loss were all flooding down her face through tearful anguish. It broke my heart. She rolled her head in my direction, sobbing uncontrollably, looking to me to rescue her. It was as if she was being ripped from my grasp. I felt so helpless and angry, sad and disappointed, hating what was but hopeful for what could be.

With Judy loaded into the ambulance, I emphatically affirmed for Judy that I would be right behind her and that she was going to be ok.

Having closed the doors and with the ambulance now pulling away from the loading zone, I turned and walked towards my car. With the emotional restraints lifted, I crumbled to my knees on the grassy median and wailed deep, gut-wrenching wails. Each cry heaving from the recesses of my being uncontrollably. It was as if every wail was desperately attempting to express the inexpressible, trying to rectify in my mind how this ongoing life storm was not only possible but could actually make sense. It was beyond my ability to reconcile. While Judy and I's life was being sifted, I was grateful that even though I could only express uncommunicable tears, God understood my unutterable groans. In this crumpled form of humanity on the grass, I felt that I had a companion in David when he wrote in his season of lament,

"I am exhausted and completely crushed.
My groans come from an anguished heart.
You know what I long for, Lord;
You hear my every sigh." (Psalm 38:8-9 NLT).

I have no conscious awareness of how long I wept on the median or who passed by and wondered in my convulsions what life predicament had reduced me to such a state. But having regained enough composure, I rose from the ground and made my way to the car.

Even though I had driven this section of I-5 in northern California many times before, this trip seemed excruciatingly longer. The harvesting of the nut groves that stretched along the interstate for miles, however, seemed poignantly symbolic. A harvest, symbolically, encompasses both provision and blessing, hope and a future, thankfulness and trust confirmed. The anticipated season of wondering and waiting was over. The time for reaping what had been planted by faith and with guarded assurance in seasons before had now grown into fruition, maturity and was ready for harvest. The prayer of petition for what was not seen had become a prayer of thankfulness for abundance.

I love the story in Mark 6 with Jesus feeding the five thousand which, by all accounts, was closer to ten to fifteen thousand people counting women and children. But in this story, the twelve disciples of Jesus were concerned that evening was approaching and this multitude was food-less. They were rightly concerned that this huge crowd would transform into a hangry crowd. In looking at an anxiously dire and impossible situation, the disciples urge Jesus to send the people away.

But Jesus, knowing the same circumstances and seeing the same crowd, wants to pull them in rather than send them away. Same circumstances, same crowd. But the disciples only seen impossibility while Jesus sees what is possible. It is all about perspective and the heart.

So, Jesus says, "You feed them."

"With what?" they asked. "We'd have to work for months to earn enough money to buy food for all these people."

Their answer wasn't wrong, it's just too small. They'd forgotten who was in their presence. The reality is that we can become so circumstantially focused that we eliminate the possi-

bility of a miracle. We see barren ground but forget the possibility of a coming harvest. In the midst of our limited
perspective, we fail to realize that God wants us to live a life so
big that He has to be in it in order for us to live out that life.

After the disciples' question and excuse, Jesus asks, "How
much bread do you have?" What a great question. Jesus didn't
ask them what they didn't have. He asked them, "How much
bread do you have?" And the question isn't an insulting question. Jesus knows they don't have enough bread to feed everyone.
He wants to see their faith level.

"Where's your faith at?"

"How much bread do you have?"

"What do you have in your hands?"

"What's in your heart?"

Our natural response is, "Whatever I have, it's not enough."

In the story, it says that after a search for food that the disciples presented Jesus with five loaves of bread and two fish. Barely
a Lunchables amount to snack on, let alone feed a mass of
people.

"Jesus told the disciples to have the people sit down in
groups on the green grass. So they sat down in groups of fifty or
a hundred." I love the details.

"Jesus took the five loaves and two fish, looked up toward
heaven, and blessed them. Then, breaking the loaves into pieces,
he kept giving the bread to the disciples so they could distribute
it to the people. He also divided the fish for everyone to share."

"They all ate as much as they wanted, and afterward, the
disciples picked up twelve baskets of leftover bread and fish. A
total of 5,000 men and their families were fed."

The summation of the story is that Jesus stepped in where
the disciples couldn't, and he met the need. The disciples weren't
able to see the "harvest" that was coming but in the hands of
Jesus, nothing is impossible.

On this familiar drive under unfamiliar circumstances, I
made the decision to trust that a harvest, a reaping of the possi-

bility of God in regard to Judy's recovery and healing was coming even though I had no visible appearance of it now.

Arriving at NeuroRestorative Granite Bay, I was struck by the initial simplicity of the facility. The one level, brick exterior resembled a 1980's extended ranch house with a two-car garage. The grounds were well manicured with fall decorations dotting the walkway to the front door. All relieving a portion of my angst that Judy would be temporarily homed in a sterile, rehabilitation center void of color and surrounded by cement.

Having checked in and had my temperature taken via COVID protocol, I was directed to Judy's room which was located at the end of the initial hallway but within eyeshot of the front desk. The interior of the facility did not fully match the "hominess" of the outside. The layout was in an "L" shape with a gathering room large enough for group activities, the physical therapy center, a large bathing/shower room, the nurse's station, and individual resident rooms. Resident artwork and pictures of group activities and holiday festivities lined the hallway walls.

Walking into Judy's room, I was taken aback by the lack of décor or attempts to make it inviting. There was one folding chair, a small dresser, closet with drawers, and a TV mounted to the wall. That was it. Not that I expected any "Welcome" banners or streamers acknowledging Judy's arrival, I had hoped for a little more than I found. Already admitted, Judy was in her bed waiting for my arrival. Her familiar hospital gown that she was transported in had been replaced with a men's X-Large t-shirt with a local professional hockey team logo on the front. Clearly not Judy's choice or style of clothing. The starkness of the room, the expanse of the hospital bed, and the oversized shirt that Judy was swimming in made her seem more fragile, displaced, and vulnerable than since her ordeal had begun.

It wasn't long after my arrival that the administrative assistant walked into the room with a book of forms that needed to be filled out and signed. Fifty-seven pages to be exact. Page after page of disclaimers, instructions, facility and staff protective declarations, media consent, resident information, insurance qualifications, medical status, and a check list of personal items. Now I consider myself to be a fairly intellectual person with an acceptable degree of smarts having obtained an MA in Intellectual Leadership. But reading through this mountain of forms and understanding all the verbiage was a challenge that left me questioning not only my mental acumen but what in the world I had signed Judy in for.

Following the administrative assistant, the therapist team appeared in the room outlining the therapy plan they envisioned for Judy. The therapy team consisted of three therapists each representing their therapy specialty…physical, occupational, and speech. The plan would be for Judy to receive physical therapy for an hour three times a week, speech and occupational therapy for an hour two times a week, and group therapy for an hour once a week. Along with therapy, Judy would receive around the clock nursing attention and visiting physician care.

With the stress of the transition on Judy's physical and emotional systems combined with the hefty amount of information presented to us, she was exhausted and easily fell asleep. Taking advantage of her nap time, I met with the facility director for further information and clarification on anything and everything I still needed to know for my sake and Judy's. My highest concern was since I would be unable to visit and be present with Judy every day, I wanted absolute certainty that she would be cared for and looked after with utmost attention on the days I was not with her. While nothing indicated that this would be the case, the thought of her lying in bed all day, uncared for, lacking personal connection was an image that I couldn't bear. Attempting to assuage my concern, the facility director assured me, as much as she could, that Judy would receive quality and personal care every day. I wanted to fully believe her, but I resolved myself to the realization that my expectation of care and daily engagement wouldn't or couldn't be met with reality. So I had to trust that the One who knew her best would meet Judy in the gaps where physical presence fell short. The facility director also gave me full permission to attend all therapy sessions when I was with Judy and once a week, I would be included in a phone consultation with the therapists, the charge nurse, facility director, and primary care physician to discuss Judy's status, progress, and concerns.

The bare closet and empty drawers were a clarion call that some essential items were needed...like clothing. Either out of my ignorance or the facility director's lack of communication, I had completely missed the important piece of information that Judy would need to wear clothes. I had become accustomed to Judy's daily attire being a hospital gown. Now, she needed actual pants and shirts like regular people. Tracking down the physical therapist, I inquired as to what she suggested would be the best clothing options given Judy's new daily regimen. Sweatpants, sweatshirts, everything loose fitting, and easy slip-on shoes was the fashion of choice. In a couple of hours, I found myself in the foreign land of the women's clothing section at a nearby department store. Over the years, I had been in the women's section many times while shopping with Judy but being the sole male in the women's section searching for appropriate clothing items alone, without her, had me feeling completely and conspicuously out of place. This feeling became even more pronounced in me as I fumbled my way through bra sizes, packs of underwear, leggings and jeggings and hurriedly tossed them into my cart as if speed was going to reduce any unwanted attention. As the items in my cart began to increase, so did the level of my perspiration. I felt way too sweaty, the lights were way too bright, my heart rate was beating way too fast for such an ordeal, and there were way too many females I was having to avoid eye contact with. The whole time I was secretly praying for God to perform another "parting of the Red Sea" and keep any and all store clerks from descending upon me asking if I needed any help. Even if I did, I wasn't about to admit it. But what dawned on me for the first time in my life was that the struggle to find appropriately fitting women's clothing was real.

"Who wears this stuff?"

"Why are all the necklines so low cut?"

"What would this match with?"

"Why is everything so tight?"

"Where are the normal clothes?"

True questions every man asks while shopping in the women's department.

The truer reality that found its place alongside the other unquestionable truths of my life as I straddled the chasm between the blouses rack and the bra section was that while I'm not sure who women's apparel was designed to fit, I know for certain that it's not the average sized, middle to older aged woman.

In examining the contents of my cart, I quickly surmised that leggings and jeggings were not going to do the trick. While somewhat elastic, they would be too difficult to get on and off and so they were uncaringly discarded to the closest shelf. In their place, I decided that regular sweatpants, larger, roomier sweatshirts in Judy's favorite colors and men's t-shirts with more of a box cut than form fitting were better choices.

Feeling accomplished and confident in my selections, I, with less confidence, placed all my items on the check-out conveyor belt. As the employee began scanning each individual barcode, I blurted out without provocation or cause, "It's all for my wife." But as if that wasn't enough, the next words tumbled out, "Even the men's shirts." Why did I have to say anything at all? Why did it matter? The employee hadn't questioned me or even neces-sarily made the connection between myself and the particular clothing items passing in front of her but I felt that she needed to know so as to remove any suspicion or doubt.

Then, as if to make everything understandable and provide closure for the employee's sake, I stated, "She had a stroke and is in rehab." The employee, giving all appearances of having ignored my conversation or to move beyond any uncomfortable angst she was experiencing, placed the receipt in the bag and robotically responded, "Thanks for shopping with us. Have a nice day."

With that, I claimed my items and headed back to Judy, nerves shaken but victorious.

The Fall season was rapidly reclaiming more daylight, giving evidence that the upcoming winter solstice was approaching. Which meant that the newest rhythm of life had my "visiting" days bookended with increasing darkness. My plan was to walk into Judy's room no later than 9:00am on Mondays, Wednesdays, and Saturdays. Therefore, I needed to be backing out of my driveway by 6:00am to make the drive in time. I stayed until after supper which finished up around 6:00pm, putting me back in my driveway before 9:30 at night. Tuesdays were full meeting days at the church that I needed to be present for. Thursday and Fridays were focused on prepping all teams and being operationally set for Sunday. Then Sunday, with two full morning gatherings, I was on the church campus from 7:00am until 2:00pm. Usually one of the first in and the last out. It was my role and I carried it with full responsibility. But this new pace of life left little space to breathe. Breathing and rest for me would have to wait. Not the best prescription for self-care.

Judy and I were told that timing was critical as it pertained to her therapy and the possibility of positive outcomes and restored function to the deficit side of her body. The window for the highest chance of recovery occurs within one to three months after the stroke. It was in these ninety days that we were encouraged to expect the most improvement. This was all due to the neuroplasticity of the brain. Neuroplasticity is when the brain cells have the capacity to regenerate and re-route brain communication around the damaged or deadened parts of the brain caused by the stroke. Therapy and repetitive exercises could essentially rewire the brain and remap the brain to construct new neurological highways to compensate for loss. For all intents and purposes, the brain goes into road construction mode. And like road construction season in the Midwest, you've got three months between winter's thaw and winter's return to get it all done and so every road has detour signs, heavy equipment, and inconvenient closures that drivers must frustratingly and tenaciously navigate. It was the same for Judy's brain. The frustrating and tenacious work to navigate through this "road construction" season was vital to recovery.

Therapy started immediately. The effects of a stroke on the body are cruel and callous. For Judy, the stroke, combined with the bed ridden regimen of the past month, had completely erased her ability to control her core. She had zero strength or muscle control to hold herself up in a sitting position. Added to that, she had lost cognitive awareness of her instability. So, if she was positioned upright, she was unable to control or determine where or if she was falling over if support was removed. This became ground zero for PT. They were going to focus entirely on getting Judy sitting and standing.

I am convinced that we take the wonder of physical movement, the freedom of immediate mobility, and the unconscious awareness of our strength for granted until it all becomes restricted or taken away. Prior to September 4, 2021, Judy's mobility, aside from the normal small aches and pains that accompany getting older, was as agile and free as any normal, active person of her age. Now, seeing her positioned on the PT bench, needing 100% support to sit up, the inability to lift her head straight, forcing a crooked smile in order to fend off breaking into tears, struggling to follow simple instructions and imitating easy bodily movements were incomprehensible.

Judy's determination was unquestionable but her insecurities and the constant reminders of her deficits and limitations were reflected in her eyes. With each miss, she would look at me for support and encouragement. And I readily and enthusiastically, sometimes through the emotions cracking in my voice, would encourage her to keep going. At several points as she concentrated on the present instructions, I needed to turn away and force control of my emotions for fear of falling completely apart in front of her. That was unacceptable in the moment.

An immediate and clear principle of physical therapy that was communicated from the outset was that there was no failure in PT. The therapist would gently cup Judy's face in her hands as each PT session was set to begin and remind her, "failure doesn't exist in this room. We have misses, not failures. We have opportunity for growth, not failure." As this mantra was repeated with each session, it not only became a powerful infusion of hope for Judy but for me as well.

Life has an unrelenting way of defining our mistakes as failures and we're punished as a consequence. From our earliest days in elementary school, our ability to perform and succeed is graded from an "A" to "Failure." A's are rewarded and F's are punished. Incorrect choices and wrong decisions are labeled as failures and punishment is handed out accordingly. As we grow older and become adults, our mistakes can contain more radically substantial consequences and, likewise, failure is branded on us with deeper scaring. Punishment lands with a harsher, penetrating reality. Unless corralled, failure seeps into the crevices of our identity and grafts itself to who we believe we are. No longer is the mistake a failure but we are a failure. We adopt a perception of ourselves which couldn't be further from the truth. Failure left unrestrained will create a barrier between our heart and reality. Everything becomes skewed and we languish in despair and self-flagellation.

Now hear me, I'm not advocating that we deny our mistakes and misses or minimize our fails so as to ignore the consequences or avoid the acknowledgment of falling short. But rather, we reframe our mistakes, misses, and fails into opportunities for growth, advancement, and greater clarity on our shortcomings and where we need to courageously face restoration. We embrace our misses and fails not as a failure but as an undeterred warrior determined to lean in, show up, and overcome. It's about mindset and identity.

With a floor length mirror positioned directly in front of her for Judy to gauge her posture, a physical therapist behind her to stabilize Judy from falling over and two therapists in front of her on either side, Judy was instructed to reach out with her right hand, grab a small plastic hoop, reach across her body and give it to the therapist on her left. Judy's left arm laying limp and motionless next to her. After doing this several times, with several misses in her attempts, the therapists adjusted the positioning of their hands and Judy would need to reach further and raise her arm either higher or lower than the previous turn in order to transfer the hoop to the therapist. This was an extreme exercise in hand/eye coordination, core strengthening, and muscle control. It was simultaneously an extreme reminder of the deficits we were dealing with.

"How can this be my wife?"

"When will Judy's brain click and we'll pick up where we left off?"

"When will her split functioning/non-functioning body sync into one being?"

Each question was another prayer request. Another petition for God to act, respond, or move on Judy's behalf. Yet, again, nothing. At least from the outward appearance of Judy's condition nothing was changing. I had to keep reminding myself that there was still time. It was way too early to give up hope. In a sense, I was giving God more time as well.

The onset of exhaustion after each therapy session required Judy to take a nap. As her body recouped and caught its breath, I sat on the folding chair and watched her. Drifting into sleep myself for a few moments at a time, I would be awakened by her breathing or a random noise in the hallway and refix my attention on the best part of me lying in her bed. After an hour or two of rest, Judy would be roused from sleep for another round of therapy, a vitals check, or mealtime.

One oasis of love in this new chapter was that a dear friend made copies of roughly 30-40 photos of friends and family and gave them to me along with a sign that read "Judy's Team." On my next visit, I pinned all the photos on the walls around her room. The photos literally wallpapered her space. It was a visible, tangible clear reminder to Judy that she had an army of supporters rooting for her. She was not alone. Judy's team was actively present.

It didn't take long to find ourselves in a rhythm with this new schedule. While it was grueling and exhausting, it was our current life. The most torturous part of our routine was every evening as the clock determined my time to leave. Needing to make the three-hour drive back home dictated my departure time. Judy's supper arrived to her room between 5:00 and 5:30pm each evening. Due to her inability to completely, independently feed herself, I would assist in the process of trying to make sure that more of her meal made it to her mouth than not. I wasn't always the best or most accurate help, but I gave it my full effort. Once she had had enough or her meal was completed, it was time to leave.

I hated leaving.

I hated knowing that she would be left alone.

I hated realizing that there would be a number of days when I wouldn't see her.

I hated feeling guilty for walking out of the room and attempting to live a life "separate" from her.

I hated the drive through Sacramento traffic back home to an empty space.

I hated having to turn down her emotional requests for me to stay longer.

Every departure tore at my heart and raised the level of anxiety and fear in Judy. Sleeping through the night was no longer in existence for her. She now slept in spurts which meant that for intermittent hours of darkness, she would lay in bed awake, alone. Giving space for her mind to contemplate every scenario, to exaggerate every fear, and to engage in the mental battle between despair and hope. Sleep was no longer enjoyable or inviting for Judy. It was a wrestling match of emotions, intermingled with moments of rest.

My leaving also meant that Judy would need to endure the next day's therapy without my presence and encouragement. Not that my presence was a necessity but having been a team together up to this point in our lives, we were still a team and relied on each other. In my absence, she would have to fight through it with her own grit and determination. The willpower to dig deep and face the monumental task of facing her circumstances would need to come from within and from a deeper well of faith.

One of the most often spiritual phrases recited to us through card or text for the intent of encouragement were the words, "God will not give us more than we can handle." A statement loosely based on Paul's words in 1 Corinthians 10:13. But not only is that phrase not contextually correct, it's not true. In 1 Corinthians 10:13, the context is dealing with temptation and being swayed into sin. Paul says, "And God is faithful; he will not let allow the temptation to be more than you can stand. When you are tempted, he will show you a way out so that you can endure." The instruction is that temptation and sin do not have to have the final word on our decisions. God does give us a way out rather than giving in.

But more importantly, the phrase that "God will not give us more than we can handle" simply isn't true. It's a spiritually naïve way to live. It's a living with our head in the sand attempt at daily existence. God clearly gives us more than we can handle, and it's called life. Every day we are faced with the potential of more than we can handle or carry. The unpredictable, the unexpected, the "less-than-ideal," the traumatic and tragic can slap us in the face without warning at any moment. With the intent being that it drives us to Jesus in dependence. Because life does give us more than we can handle, we lean into the power and presence that God provides to navigate the insurmountable waves that strike us. What would be the purpose of hope, of belief, of perseverance, of reaching out and grabbing ahold of the hand of Jesus if we were promised to never encounter the shit storms of life? It's due to the fact that life often sucker punches us and unrelentingly continues to pummel us when we're down that we cling to hope, belief, and tighten our grip on the hand of Jesus. As life rolls over us, we plant our feet on our firm foundation of faith and we stand and fight.

At some point in the early days of Judy's rehab, she adopted Rachel Platten's "Fight Song" as her PT theme song. The therapists came to know this and so they would blast it as Judy was putting in the work.

"This is my fight song
Take back my life song
Prove I'm alright song
My power's turned on
Starting right now I'll be strong
I'll play my fight song
And I don't really care if nobody else believes
'Cause I've still got a lot of fight left in me."

As the song crescendoed into that chorus, the floodgate of tears would open for Judy and offer her an extra burst of motivation to fight through each exercise. She definitely had a lot of fight left in her.

The ongoing unsettling reality for me was that when I was away from Judy, I was unable to keep an eye on her welfare and condition. Anything less than her absolute care was unacceptable. This was a proverbial hill that I was willing to die on for her. Not that I was untrusting of the staff's care for Judy but, in reality, I guess I was. I simply had reservations that they could or would provide the protection and concern that I felt was warranted. This was unfortunately made apparent to me after a visit.

Having left Judy, I wove my way through the Sacramento

traffic and headed north on I-5 towards home. About halfway
through my three-hour drive, I received a call from the rehab
facility. Since it was approaching 8:00pm and the facility rarely
called, this was more than slightly unnerving. Unable to answer
the phone as I was driving, I waited for the chime of a voicemail
and aimed for the nearest exit. Arriving at a safe location and
with my adrenaline racing, I pressed play to listen to the
recorded voicemail,

"Hi Eric, this is the nurse from NeuroRestorative Granite
Bay. I just wanted to let you know that a couple minutes after
you left from the building, your wife fell from the bed.

I just wanted to let you know that. There is nothing serious
to worry about. She

has a little bruise on her upper lip. But we've already ordered
an x-ray for her in the morning."

I immediately pressed the redial button as my protective
anger began surging through

my bodily system. Reeling from this snippet of information,
I needed clarity and answers as this seemed so incomprehensible
to me. With the nurse answering my call, I dove in with questions and unapologetic frustration as to how this could have
happened.

The explanation for what occurred was when Judy attempted
to roll over from her right to her left, she grabbed the bed rail to
pull herself over. As she did so, the bed rail gave way and Judy
rolled out of the bed and onto the floor. As a result, her face hit
the floor....

"Wait! Hold on! Her face hit the floor?" I asked in shock.
My unrestrained anger clearly not matching his apparent "this
happens every day" casual depiction of events. The nurse
continued by affirming my question that Judy's face had indeed
hit the floor but that there was nothing to worry about. I failed
to resonate with his lack of worry. As he had stated in the voicemail, she simply had a bruise on her upper lip and an x-ray on
her head would be taken in the morning.

Now I needed to know the bigger question…how did this happen? Without hesitation, the nurse's first explanation for what caused Judy's fall was that I had failed to secure her bed rail when I left. I was appalled that I was the first excuse for Judy's accident. With no hiding the exasperation in my voice, I confronted the nurse over the absurdity of his statement. The railing was up when I left and the last person to have had their hands on it was a staff member who raised it after Judy completed her supper. I, intentionally, made sure before leaving that Judy was secure and peacefully at ease for the night. There was no way that I would have left her vulnerable to a fall.

Having voiced my frustration over the accusation, the nurse recanted and said that it was possible that a staff member had repositioned Judy and failed to lock the railing in place. Regardless, the weightier concern was Judy and her physical condition.

After consulting with my daughter, Erika, we decided that there was nothing I could do that night for Judy and since the nurse reassured me that they would be keeping a close eye on her throughout the night (which didn't make me feel very confident), I continued with my journey home with the plan to return to the Rehab facility the following morning.

Judy's face had clearly taken the brunt of the fall. Her upper lip was swollen, her lower lip was swollen and bruised as she had bit it in the fall, and there was slight bruising on the side of her face. Her right shoulder was also sore as a result of colliding with the floor as well. Her appearance clearly called into question the lack of severity expressed by the nurse the night before. I immediately tracked down the nurse on duty to receive a follow up report. She informed me that the x-ray had already been performed before my arrival and that the results were negative for any brain or head injuries. Thankfully, the fall hadn't broken any teeth or Judy's nose. The x-ray report was good news but hardly relieved my anger over the incident. I realized that in settings such as Judy's with limited and overworked staff and numerous opportunities for accidents to happen that it wasn't beyond the realm of possibility for an accident to occur to her. But it was still unacceptable.

While the fall was troubling enough, it was the scare and unprotection instilled in Judy's psyche and now fully evidenced through her expression that ripped at my heart the most. Once again, the sense of my own ineptness felt suffocating. I couldn't protect her from a stroke. I couldn't alleviate or eliminate her steps of recovery. I couldn't guarantee her safety. As much as I so desperately wanted to, I couldn't assure her of painless days and accident-free nights. I couldn't confirm when she'd be home again. I couldn't promise that the worst was behind her. *I couldn't.* The reality of those words stung like pelting hail on my innermost perception of adequacy, masculinity, and protective responsibility. I had vowed to protect her and yet at her most vulnerable moments, I couldn't.

So once again, as was now becoming my daily if not hourly resignation, "God, you know how I feel. This doesn't seem fair or right but I can't make it better. I can't do enough. So, I place Judy in your hands again."

The simple act of letting go of what we cannot control and placing it in the hands of God provides just enough space in the tension of what is to regain our footing. While I can't, He can. While I'm undeniably weak, He is undeterrably strong. My frailty, His faithfulness.

October's increased presence brought the turning of leaves, foggier morning drives, and cooler temperatures. It also offered the realization that winter was around the corner. Thankfully, winter in northern California is wonderfully mild compared to other notoriously unrelenting and punishingly cold climates. We, Californians, actually look forward to winter with anticipation as it provides a much desired respite from the scorching summer heat and the hope of much needed precipitation after months of drought. But the change in the weather meant that we would be embarking on a change of seasons as well.

Fall was Judy's favorite time of the year. She loved the transformation of the summer greens to the vibrant fall yellows, oranges, and reds. She loved the fragrances carried in the autumn air. She always had. Many autumn afternoons after our college courses were done for the day, Judy would suggest we take a drive to the nearby park for an afternoon date. Once there, she would enthusiastically revel in the surroundings of tall, fluffy plumes of pampas grass, the bright red sumac leaves, and the crunching of elm and maple leaves under her feet. For Judy, autumn was a season of renewal even though by nature's stand-point everything was becoming more dormant. She breathed deeply of life.

As therapy was directing their focus more and more on Judy being able to regain her core strength in sitting up, they positioned her in her wheelchair for longer periods of time. They wanted her out of her bed and in an upright posture. This meant that Judy was free to be transported beyond the confines of her room and outside to the patio.

The wheelchair offered a limited but opportunistic means of escape. With the head support in place, the chest strap snuggly secured across Judy's torso, and her feet firmly on the footrests we would make a break for it. As I maneuvered the wheelchair past the therapy gym, past the watchful eye of the administrative assistant, past the large common room and over the threshold into the fresh air of freedom as Judy suppressed squeals of excite-ment, it did carry the feeling of a prison break. Not that I have any actual idea what that would feel like. But for Judy, getting outside was heaven.

Her crooked smile was never as luminous as when the warmth of the sun touched her face and the breeze wafted through her hair. We'd use this outdoor gift of freedom to Face-Time our kids, compete over who could spot the birds first, and simply hold hands and imaginarily transport ourselves to a much different location and time void of a stroke's cruelty.

Time would pass too quickly and before long, the strenuous activity of sitting up would reach its max and Judy would

request to be returned to her bed. Everything was a process and
required multiple hands. Transferring Judy from her wheelchair
to the bed involved two staff and a Hoyer hydraulic patient lift.
The way the Hoyer Lift operated was that a comfortable sling
was placed under the person that needed help being moved. In
Judy's situation, the sling was pre-set in the wheelchair prior to
Judy being placed on top of it. The sling was then attached
securely to hooks on a swivel bar that was attached at the top of
the lift. The hydraulic arm lifted the person into the air and in
the desired direction they needed to go. For Judy, the staff
personnel would then maneuver the Hoyer so that Judy was
dangling securely over her bed and then lowered onto her
mattress.

This process was necessary for every transfer from the bed
to the wheelchair and back again. It became so routine that the
Hoyer lost all of its unnerving presence. In fact, the Hoyer Lift
rolled into the room became synonymous with freedom,
opportunity, hope for improvement, and recovery. Not that
Judy and I began to salivate like Pavlov's trained dogs when we
heard the sound of the Hoyer's wheels turning in our direction, but it definitely made our pulse quicken and anticipation
rise.

Being physically restricted to only two locations...bed and
wheelchair...was beyond discouraging for Judy. It was difficult
enough for her to mentally grasp the depth of her deficits and
the magnitude of her journey to recovery. But to add insult to
injury was the fact that Judy was totally at the mercy and availability of the nursing staff or therapists for any physical movement. If therapy wasn't scheduled for the day and if the nurses
were understaffed and overworked, Judy was confined to her bed
without options. On the flipside, if Judy's stay in her wheelchair
was beyond what she felt she could endure, she had no other
choice but to wait until a team of personnel were available to
make the transfer. It wasn't intentional by the staff, it's just the
way it was. Her change in location was controlled by their

convenience. Even if I was present and able to help, I was forbidden for insurance and liability issues.

I can't begin to imagine the mental and emotional incarceration that Judy must have felt. Half of her body failing to respond and act in conjunction with the other half of her body while the entirety of her mind knew it. Her memory fully intact so as to easily recall the fluidity and independence of being able to physically move about without a second thought but now being helplessly constricted as if her own body had revolted and staged a coup against her mind and muscles. The ever-present reminder that prior to September 4, Judy's mobility was completely at-will but now, without the aid of others, mobility was non-existent.

Even though this was her current sentence, Judy didn't complain, get angry, or lash out in frustration. She simply would occasionally be overcome with emotion attributing itself to the notion of being a burden and grieving her losses. While she never voiced it, I could tell by her expression and interaction from those in charge that Judy had become uncharacteristically insecure. Over the years of my life with Judy, I knew that she was not the most adventurous and definitely did not throw caution to the wind but she was admirably secure in who she was.

This should not be interpreted that Judy was in any way arrogant, pompous, or conceited. Not at all. She firmly knew her identity. She knew who she was in Christ and that identification made all the difference for her. There was no room to pretend to be different. Judy embraced her strengths and understood her weaknesses. But in the aftermath of suffering a stroke and the ongoing processing of that reality, it was as if she had also suffered an identity crisis. Not that she now questioned her position or salvation in Christ or that that in any way had been adjusted or altered because it hadn't, but it was as if she lost sight of being a person of value. While relishing absolute spiritual dependence on Jesus for all that she was and needed, being absolutely dependent on everyone else now had crushed her security.

Judy's demeanor seemed anxious and nervous around others. In the presence of her therapists and nurses she longingly looked to understandably receive a daily injection of positive affirmation or encouraging approval while, at the same time, voicing a self-defeated assessment that any affirmation or approval was unwarranted. The negative aspects of her condition and status of recovery were becoming more prominent in her communication. It was not as if she was giving up. By no means was that the case but her positivity was definitely waning in the struggle.

A joyous occasion that boosted Judy's spirits was when her mom and both sisters came to visit for a few days. Knowing the dates for their visit were soon approaching, I noticed Judy's sense of anxiousness rising once more. She voiced her uneasiness and uncertainty of being able to handle having visitors, even dear ones such as her family. As I pressed into the reasoning behind why she was feeling this way, Judy opened up and lamented how disappointing it would be for them to see her in her present condition. She projected onto them a sense of disapproval that she was not better or, at least, not more along the road to recovery than she was. Judy relayed that she was self-conscious about her clarity of speech, her inability to feed herself, and the reality of needing to be changed with them in the room. This was not how she wanted her mom and sisters to see her. I loved the tenderness expressed through her admission. Quickly and rather forcefully, I assured Judy that none of those projected attitudes would be even remotely present in her mom, Jane, or Nancy. They were coming to see her for their own heart's sake and not with a regimented recovery expectation. I also reassured her that knowing her mom and sisters as well as I did, that the very last thing Judy needed to be concerned about was her deficits and disabilities being a disappointment for them. The three of them would eagerly and lovingly jump in and help or watch or step out of the room as needed. They, as I unquestioningly and without concern knew they would be, were caringly sensitive to Judy, her condition, and surroundings.

Marge, Jane, and Nancy were able to see, firsthand, Judy in all her rehab elements. They sat in on her therapy sessions, helped with Judy's feedings, and spent time laughing and reflecting on life. On one afternoon, group therapy engaged in painting pumpkins. Judy enthusiastically dove in. She chose her colors and had an artistic plan in mind for what she wanted her pumpkin to look like. Each stroke of the brush added a splash of color to the pumpkin's design. Unfortunately, the stroke's heinous robbery of Judy's hand/eye coordination made directing the brush to achieve the artist's intentions very difficult. Mentally imagined shapes became indistinguishable blobs. Colors were added layer upon layer, turning reds and yellows and blues into swaths of gray. As attempts were repeatedly made to correct the overall appearance, they only served to worsen the outcome. With every unsuccessful brushstroke, tears began to stream down Judy's cheeks. Her pumpkin wasn't turning out how she wanted at all. At one point through her tears, she blurted out in frustration and embarrassment, "This isn't what I want. I want it to be better."

That frustrated and embarrassed outburst conveyed more than disappointment over a therapeutic painting exercise. Judy was vocalizing her pain from a deep internal well of sadness. None of it was what she wanted, at all. The reason I mention that brief incident in time is because it encapsulated every emotion for Judy and me in that season. What could have been an encouraging, enjoyable, segment of life was, instead, discouraging, defeating, and a visual reminder that life can literally turn on a dime with traumatic invasion. Life, without respect for persons, can indiscriminately and unsympathetically introduce suffering and the questioning over the meaning and purpose of that life.

Suffering and trauma do not remove meaning and purpose for living but they can raise doubts on what we believed before with absoluteness. As long as our daily existence goes unobstructed, we cling to our belief structures and systems without question. But when our daily rhythm is rudely and uninvitedly detoured, a natural and needed introspection occurs which questions and re-evaluates the foundational beliefs we've pre-determined we're anchored to.

The truth is that life has meaning and purpose regardless of the circumstances, no matter how joyful or perilous, comforting or traumatic, encouraging or disappointing. As long as we have breath, we have purpose. As long as we have another day, we have meaning. In the throes of trauma and despair, that can be much easier said than lived out, but it is still true and needs to be revisited often even when we don't fully believe it in the moment.

As Judy's mind and therapy sessions waged war to regain mobility and lost physical ground, her body attempted to sabotage her progress. One such act of sabotage, as the list continued to grow, was that her body had a difficult time regulating sodium levels resulting in either hyponatremia or hypernatremia. For a healthy, normal individual, sodium levels fall within the range of 135-145 milliequivalents per liter. Hyponatremia occurs when sodium in the body falls below the 135 marker. The cause for hyponatremia is that there is too much water or fluid build up in the body. The kidneys simply aren't processing the fluid out through normal means. Some of the primary symptoms of hyponatremia include nausea, confusion, muscle twitches, and low blood pressure. For a stroke patient such as Judy, hyponatremia becomes sinister as it mimics a stroke. Facial muscles droop, speech becomes excessively slurred, mental confusion worsens, and blood pressure bottoms out leaving the patient lethargic and unresponsive.

On the flip side, hypernatremia is when there is too much sodium in the blood system and not enough water. In other words, there has been too much water loss and/or sodium gain creating a dangerous imbalance. Some of the familiar signs of hypernatremia are excessive thirst, fatigue, muscle spasms, and confusion. The primary signal-teller between the two conditions is excessive thirst. With hypernatremia, you can't get enough fluids to quench your thirst.

Added to Judy's list of bodily sabotages were urinary tract infections. Due to her incontinence and sedentary condition, she was unfortunately more susceptible to UTIs. Her body couldn't process necessary functions normally and so her system rebelled. Judy's UTIs were mostly contained within her kidneys and bladder. The incontinence was extremely embarrassing and aggravating for her. Judy hated being so needy and requiring that type of personal attention several times a day. Not only did she have no control over when she went, she also had no feeling or awareness of the need to go or that she had already gone. This situation left her as a prime candidate for repeated infections. The troubling aspect of a UTI is that it mimicked sodium symptoms…confusion, muscle twitching, nausea, shaking and chills. Without a test being performed, it was difficult to tell the difference by the mere appearances.

The hardship created by either imbalanced sodium levels or a UTI is that it required Judy to be hospitalized, usually for several days at a time. Because her physical condition was so compromised there were combined domino effects. It wasn't only imbalanced sodium levels that needed to be regulated again but it would simultaneously affect her swallowing ability which meant that she would need an IV to stay hydrated and nourished which meant longer hospitalization to regain the ability to eat and swallow again. Domino after domino after domino. The most difficult aspect of each hospital stay was the setback it would create for her. Having taken three steps forward through her therapy and daily rhythm, she'd slip two steps back while in the hospital. It took such an emotional and physical toll on her. Upon every hospital discharge (4 at this point in time), it seemed like we were starting over in so many disappointing ways. The hardship was daunting.

* * *

Judy and I certainly weren't unfamiliar with hardship prior to her stroke and its aftermath. It was just different but no less daunting. Having spent close to thirty years in ministry, we know from personal experience that full-time pastoral church work is not for the faint of heart. The responsibilities, challenges, needs, expectations, time demands, and pressures, all while attempting to do life, raise children, fight for a healthy marriage, and maintain a semblance of balance through it all can be overwhelming.

Judy and I pastored in three different churches. For the record, I purposefully mentioned Judy as a pastor with me because even though she wasn't officially conferred that title, she carried a significant ministry load with me over the years. She energetically and skillfully led teams, created curriculum, developed ministries, counseled, mentored, organized events, and the list could go on. And she did all of that while homeschooling our kids for the majority of those years as well.

But each of those three churches was as uniquely different as our three kids. Each having their own personality, strengths, and weaknesses. Within each, there were people that we came to deeply love and who maintained friendships with us long after we had moved on. People who not only became friends but committed teammates who joined us in picking up the mantel of leadership and ministry responsibility for the sake of a larger call on their lives. Thinking back as the names of those individuals run through my mind in this moment fills me with gratitude.

The first church we pastored was in rural northwest Wisconsin. I was young and inexperienced. An introvert thrust into the extrovert arena of preaching, teaching, and leading. All of which required verbal engagement and stepping beyond my known comfort zones at that time. Thankfully, this small group of people embraced me and my inexperience with patience and grace. Judy won their affection easily. So, it didn't take long for our congregants to become family. The track record of pastors, prior to my arrival, wasn't the best, however. When the call came inviting me to be the pastor, the church had been in existence for only ten years, and I was to be their fifth pastor. Doing the math, they were averaging a new pastor ever two years. While that didn't bode well for my long-term job security, some needed turnover had occurred, people who needed to leave had left, and new leadership was in place. From their position, it felt like a fresh start. But being naïve and inexperienced offered me the opportunity and a little longer leash to try new things and make mistakes, recover, and grow.

Despite being a small rural community with a population of 2000, the church encountered a season of growth. New families, new ministry ventures, and an openness to move in new directions, coupled with the favor of God, put Judy and I on an almost ten year run with that church family. It was a blessed season for us and our kids. The space to learn, make mistakes, and grow allowed me to also develop my budding leadership skills. Being assertive and confrontive or leading with confidence were not my forte at that point in my life but I quickly found my leadership footing. All the while, Judy was diligent and creative in developing and building children's ministries, small groups, bible studies, and being the vital connecter that she was.

After almost ten years, I felt God stirring my heart to make a change. So, in a move that could have only been orchestrated by God, we uprooted our family and transitioned to a suburb of Milwaukee with the intention of planting a new church. Upon arriving on the scene, we were welcomed by a total of 13 people. That was our entire group. Thirteen people, no kids except our three. Unfamiliar territory, unfamiliar faces, and unfamiliar challenges. The familiar rhythm of our lives, the safety of our daily routines, and the comfort of people we'd grown to deeply love doing life with were gone. To barrow the famous phrase, we weren't *in Kansas anymore.*

With no church building at our disposal, we were granted access to meet weekly in a school gymnasium. As uninviting and bland as an elementary school gym can be, it became our Sunday morning gathering spot for the next five years. Within a short amount of time, our small tribe of 13 began to grow. Every Sunday, a committed team of volunteers transformed that vast room with its cement block walls, basketball hoops, and parquet floor into a sanctuary with chairs, audio and lighting systems, fresh brewed coffee, greeters, and host teams. The lunchroom became our kids' space and the library, our nursery. We made it work and again, God showed His favor on this endeavor, and we encountered, over and over, the wonder of transformed lives. Despite our location, lack of typical church aesthetics, purposeful avoidance of being programmatic, that group of thir-teen mushroomed to close to 200.

While everything on the surface looked extremely positive, internally things were unraveling. There became a growing dissension at the Governing Board level. Not everyone in leader-ship was happy or in favor of the direction the church was headed or with the type of people we were reaching as if there were any "wrong" types. My leadership abilities, giftings, and personality were all called into question. Even though our Sunday morning gatherings were growing and there was an expressed hunger for the moving of God, the same disgruntled leaders were dissatisfied with the style of music, women in roles of leadership, the type of preaching, and the need for the lights and sound and they voiced their opinions regularly. The more I held my ground on the values I believed in and what we were doing, the more contentious the Board Meetings became. One bullying board member even told me, "I've outlasted every other pastor, I'll outlast you." I came to dread Board Meetings. So much so that in the days leading up to them, I would lose my appetite. The stress of it all was beginning to take a noticeable effect on me.

Since this is not the place to unpack and process all that happened, the shortened version of the story is that I was put in an unwinnable position and made the decision to resign. I was devastated. Judy and I had sacrificed and wholeheartedly given five years of our lives to birthing this church and seeing the hand of God produce life and community and then it was over.

As the news leaked out regarding my resignation, confusion arose, and questions began to pour into Board members from congregants. My resignation at that point in time didn't make sense. As a result, support for the Board plummeted. False accusations about myself, Judy, and even my kids were made by some Board members to substantiate the reasoning for and necessity of my decision.

My last Sunday leading that church was on Easter Sunday, 2005.

Looking back now from the vantage point of time and experience, I recognize that I didn't handle every conversation or meeting well nor lead with wisdom. I allowed things to become personal and my propensity for responding defensively was not an asset. But the truth was that I was crushed. Every ounce of confidence in my preaching ability, calling, leadership capacity, and spiritual vitality was drained from me. I wasn't sleeping. My weight had dropped to 130 pounds. Emails became like toxic poison to my nervous system and had to be ignored. I had zero energy to invest in my marriage or my kids. Out of need, Judy stepped up even more than usual to cover for the gaps at home that I had created. The heaviness of the season was real for all the Foust family. None of us escaped unscathed.

With being a pastor all that I knew up to that point in my career, the only option I figured I had to provide for my family and move forward was to find another church to pastor, which I did. It was in Michigan. They were nice people and heartily embraced us but, unsuspectingly to them, I was a mess. They expressed their readiness for change and a new season of church life and so I rode in as a proverbial knight on a white horse giving all appearances of being the anticipated leader but underneath that armor, I was hemorrhaging profusely. It was just that nobody knew it.

Maybe it was due to the initial adrenaline rush of being the new man in a new place as I was able to step in and actively fulfill my required duties and responsibilities. But I couldn't sustain it. Even with a small staff able to carry portions of the ministry load, I was suffocating internally. My sense of personal value and worth was depleted. My identity was in shambles. Physically, I was showing up, but the fuel tank was empty. I didn't know who I was anymore. Familiarity with my position and routine enabled me to weekly keep pumping out what was asked of me but that was all.

Added to that reality, Judy and I had taken a sizeable pay cut in going to Michigan and given the housing crisis at the time, we sold our Wisconsin home for a loss which created unavoidable financial stress. Our income shortage was no fault of the church. They provided for us as best they could, but our personal financial pit only grew deeper. That quicksand existence forced us to make the difficult decision that Judy needed to quit homeschooling our kids and find work. It was the right decision at the time but compounded my own sense of guilt and despair over my inability to provide. I felt stuck in all facets of life.

The totality of everything unraveling in my personal world combined with my ineptness at managing the ongoing daily pastoral responsibilities that needed to be covered only served to spin me into depression and shame. A lethal combination. My introverted personality didn't work to my advantage either as I recoiled more and more into my internal, isolated world. Rather than reaching out, I shut down. My secret mental unhealth pressed me into the shadowed crevices of life. I was present but absent. I preferred to avoid people rather than engage as I had zero capacity to resolve problems, counsel, or confront…not a good situation for a pastoral position calling for in-person connection. As my perception of reality became increasingly skewed, my unmet needs for affirmation, acknowledgement, purpose, identity, and value went sideways with the result being that my life imploded but the debris field was wide. Position lost. Integrity crushed. Shame deepened. Family disrupted. Depression compounded. Sin revealed.

The truth is that I violated our marriage covenant by having an affair. As I put that sentence into permanent print, I do so with some trepidation that that admission might shift the perspective of this story away from the original intent. This is Judy's story. Our lives were deeply intertwined but in this specific script of Judy's living hope in the face of her daily struggle, I play a supporting role. She is the star. But the unavoidable reality is that my dark chapter became her dark chapter as well just in differing degrees and layers of hurt. For me, as much as I still grieve my actions, decisions, choices, and the pain that was inflicted on all, I'm eternally grateful for God's restorative work in our marriage and, more specifically, in me. It's still a work in progress but it's an ongoing work through His grace.

However, what my affair unveiled, as the ugly cesspool of my sin bubbled to the surface, was my extreme struggle over the fear of disappointing others. From my earliest childhood recollection, I feared disappointing...and being a disappointment to... my parents. There was the fear of disappointing them through my behavior but there was also the fear of who I was...me... being a disappointment. Now I can't pinpoint any specific actions or parental attitudes from my parents that instilled that fear, but it was very real and imbedded deep insecurities. As I grew older, I never felt like I measured up to my peers in school or my teachers' expectations and so the comparison game had destructive consequences for me. I continually felt insecure, less than, unseen, unknown, and not capable or qualified enough. Again, no one necessarily voiced that to me but that was my internal struggle, and the clutches of that struggle were tightly wrapped around my heart and mind. When my introversion was pressed by my fear of disappointment, I would shrink into isolation, deflect my struggle through sarcasm and humor, or resort to other tactics like lying or exaggeration to cover for my self-perceived inadequacies.

Take all of that and add in the world of pastoral church ministry with its heightened expectations to be all things to all people and it was a disaster waiting to happen. The very elements I feared became reality. My behavior was disappointing to others which meant that I, in turn, was a disappointment. When life turned the vice grip and I felt pressed, stuck, and inadequate, my insecurities and fear took on a life of their own. (Side note...while remnants of my insecurities and fear still make their ugly presence felt from time to time as life gets squeezed and my response is less than stellar, I'm drawn more and more to the ocean of God's grace and forgiveness. His love sees the darkest parts of my story and covers me still.)

In my humility, I'm often reminded of the words of David...

> *Where can I go from your Spirit?*
> *Where can I flee from your presence?*
> *If I go up to the heavens, you are there;*
> *if I make my bed in the depths, you are there.*
> *If I rise on the wings of the dawn,*
> *if I settle on the far side of the sea,*
> *even there your hand will guide me,*
> *your right hand will hold me fast.*
> *If I say, 'Surely the darkness will hide me*
> *and the light become night around me,'*
> *even the darkness will not be dark to you;*
> *the night will shine like the day,*
> *for darkness is as light to you" (Psalm 139:7-12*
> *NIV).*

Even when the residual effects of shame attempt to disqualify me or discredit God's acceptance of me, I return to the truth that He is with me and that nothing in my past can separate me from His immense ocean of love.

Through it all, Judy trudged through the victories, hardships, debris, and chaos with me. Unfortunately, she bore the brunt of the pain and heartache of my isolation, poor decisions, hurt, and wrong choices. She undeservedly paid the highest price for my compromised character, wounded heart, and mental disintegration. Having every reason to bail on the trajectory of our marriage and life based exclusively on me, she chose to stay. Judy made the decision that "for better, for worse" was a vow that she could not walk away from. She chose forgiveness. I'm eternally grateful.

Out of the scorched earth rubble, new life would begin to sprout. Tilling and preparing that scorched earth soil to be receptive to producing life again took time and effort. It required intentionality in planting new seeds of behaviors, thinking, and healing. The soil of our hearts required repeated, unrestrained, and sincere tearful precipitation. For new life to not only sprout but thrive, it also called for humble, transparent, truthful conversations with counselors, covenant friends, and each other that gave no pretense of hiding by me. I submitted to intense accountability, the owning of my mistakes, and purposeful weeding of my heart to rip out the roots of my dysfunction.

Judy had an undeterrable resolve to press forward. She recognized the magnitude of what was at stake and the loss that would be incurred should she quit. That was true in life and in therapy. Judy wasn't about to give up or give in. At any point, it could have been easy for her to decide that the effort wasn't worth it. That it was too hard, too insurmountable, too disheartening to make up lost ground…in marriage, in life, in recovery.

Too often the choice to bail out rather than put in the work required for restoration or recovery is the opted for decision. It's easier to run than face the mountain in front of us. It's easier to seek an escape rather than do the courageous work of rebuilding trust, re-establishing honesty, and redefining life out of the ruins. It's easier to allow current deficits to atrophy than exercise the cerebral shift for change and restructure. On the other hand, to stay, when safe to do so as not all circumstances are, is an act of bravery. To climb the mountain of restoration takes undaunted determination. Putting in the hard work of recovery can instill perseverance as a legacy for the next generation. Knowing the hardships of life and the need to press forward rather than quit, the Apostle Paul offers this encouragement, "So let's not get tired of doing what is good. At just the right time we will reap a harvest of blessing if we don't give up" (Galatians 6:9 NLT). It's clear from Paul's exhortation that perseverance precedes the blessing. There is the requirement to stay in the fight long enough for the end result to be revealed.

The physical therapists were insistent that Judy became increasingly independently mobile. While standing required extra attention and help, they would brace themselves on either side and lift her to an upright position, allowing her to engage the muscles and put weight on her legs for a several seconds. Even though she was unstable, and her legs didn't always want to cooperate, the fact that she was standing put a smile on Judy's face and she reveled in the affirmation.

Another step towards independence called for Judy to learn how to maneuver her wheelchair down the hallway on her own. This was an extreme feat of attempted coordination. With her good right hand, she had to grip the wheel and press forward. At the same time, with her good right foot, she had to dig in her heal on the floor and pull her leg towards her. The combined action set the chair in motion. It took every ounce of willpower and energy that she had. The problem was that by only using one hand and one foot on one side of her body was that she tended to turn to the left. Like a bumper car, she'd hit the baseboard and need to redirect to the right. Once redirected, she'd inch forward, veer to the left, and be greeted by the baseboard again. The emotional toll was high.

Progress was slow and incremental but it was still progress. Judy's physical stamina had improved enough that she graduated to only needing one therapist to assist with transfers rather than two. She was able to hold her head up better and sit with a slightly more strengthened center of balance. She increased in her ability to feed herself with the aid of a mirror placed in front of her to help in gauging the location of her mouth. Progress was good.

Improvement, however, meant another impending change. A consultation was scheduled to discuss Judy's next course of action.

The conference room was small as we gathered for the consultation. All three therapists, the head nurse, the administrator, facility director, and I positioned ourselves tightly around the table. The attending physician was on the speaker phone in the middle of the table. The lack of personal space not only made me uncomfortable but added to the adrenaline increasing in my body. All of which created a self-conscious awareness that I was probably perspiring way more than I should be at the moment. I definitely wasn't friends enough with those breathing the same confined air space as me to be this close. With Judy and her condition being the topic of conversation, each person from their respective viewpoint, took their turn assessing, evaluating, and highlighting her current status, journey of improvement, and next options. But the ultimate decision maker was that Judy had reached her insurance limitation to stay at Neuro-Restorative Granite Bay. Even though Judy had responded to therapy and demonstrated signs of minimal improvement, insurance was dictating that it was time for a change. After 9 weeks of initial therapy, the next course of action for Judy was that she would be transferred to an acute rehab facility to begin phase two of her recovery process.

PART III

Enloe Rehabilitation

Most people do not possess a penchant for change. Even though change is inevitable and many times necessary, it is still something many of us do not seek out or enjoy. According to Emerson Human Capital, "We are hardwired to resist change. Part of the brain—the amygdala—interprets change as a threat and releases the hormones for fear, fight, or flight. Your body is actually protecting you from change. The pain of loss is greater than the power of gain."*

In certain circumstances, however, change is thrust upon us without recourse. It is the only option available. Therefore, we have no choice but to move in the direction of change. Besides being generally hardwired to resist change, change raises fears. It interferes with our freedom, routine, and habits, making us feel like we've lost control over our personal domain. We're no longer the captain of our ship.

Under normal circumstances, we're able to adapt to the

* (Emerson Human Capital, April 03, 2018, Chris Pennington, https://www.emersonhc.com/change-management/people-hard-wired-resist-change).

disruption of change in a reasonable amount of time. Our mental capacities are resilient enough to bounce back and establish new rhythms and, in some situations, we may even thrive more than we thought possible because of change. But for individuals who have experienced brain injury or trauma, the mind and body may interpret change as dangerous and unsafe. They feel more vulnerable and exposed. The brain sets off a figurative fire alarm sending panic throughout the entire nervous system.

That was Judy.

The necessity and intrusion of another change spun her into a tailspin of panic, moments of uncontrollable emotion, and fear. Even though this change was communicated as a productive step on the road of recovery, the fire alarm was blaringly ringing in her brain. It wasn't as if Judy loved being a resident of NeuroRestorative Granite Bay or had developed such close, personal friendships with the staff and residents that she hated to leave. It was simply change.

The decision was made to transfer Judy to Enloe Inpatient Rehabilitation Center in Chico, CA. Enloe Rehab was a highly reputable acute rehab facility that specialized in therapy for stroke, heart attack, amputee, and traumatic brain injury patients. We were told that the triune focus on speech, physical, and occupational therapies would be purposefully intense and unsympathetically difficult. The reason was to get patients home and back to a semblance of normal life again as soon as possible. The Granite Bay staff assured us that this was a necessary next good step for Judy. A huge, personal, upside for me was that Chico and Enloe Rehab were an hour and half closer to home! My driving marathons and risking life and limb in Sacramento traffic were over.

Moving day was scheduled for Tuesday, November 22. The transfer options presented to us were either medical transport or personal vehicle. Medical transport carried the least stressful handling for Judy. She would simply be moved from her bed to a gurney, placed in the ambulance, and away she'd go. The downside of this option was that it wouldn't necessarily be covered by insurance which could result in a hefty medical bill given the distance. Also, the availability of an ambulance to transfer Judy from Sacramento to Chico, given that it crossed county lines, could be an issue. For option two, moving Judy in a personal vehicle would be much cheaper but would require her to undergo the rigorous and manhandling maneuvering into a vehicle car seat. That would be no easy task given her deficits.

Option two was our option of choice. I could sense the apprehension in Judy as I packed her belongings, removed the few decorations, and unpinned every photo from her "team" wall and carefully placed them in a folder for redistribution later. Several times during this packing session, Judy asked me and needed to be reminded of how she was going to be transferred. She was seeking clarity and reassurance that she was going to be okay. All the steps necessary to move her from her bed to the wheelchair to the car were daunting and threatening in her mind. I walked her through the process and comforted her with the realities that the therapists were strong and able and that I would be with her the whole time. She needed to trust us. Much easier said than done.

Transferring Judy from her bed to the wheelchair was routine and handled with ease. Transferring her from the chair to the car seat was a different animal altogether. With the wheels locked in place, the therapists strategically placed themselves around Judy's chair while I was inside the car, ready to help steer and manipulate her into a suitable upright position in the passenger seat. Our physical placement and bodily stances resembled a distorted version of "Twister," but we were ready. The transfer demanded one swift continuous action. The therapists each firmly gripped the gait belt around Judy's waist and on the count of three, they lifted Judy from the chair and pivoted her towards the car seat. With her body now precariously situated on the edge of the car seat, I grabbed the gait belt and pulled her towards me so that she was sitting somewhat squarely in position. Judy looked small and far from comfortable but she was in the car. After a couple more readjustments, we were ready to roll. Success!

It had been almost twelve weeks since Judy and I sat side by side together in the car. The situation felt significant and special. To celebrate, we hit the drive-thru of our favorite drink location and indulged in our treasured beverages. The smile on Judy's face as she sipped her first taste expressed a feeling of freedom, of normalcy, of life as it used to be. There were still very present reminders of her condition...the need to pinch the straw as she drank so that she would not ingest too much liquid at once, the need to repeatedly prop her back up as her core still wasn't able to keep her upright, and the need for incontinence pads placed underneath her in case of any accidents. But those were secondary to the momentary celebration that we were enjoying. For the next 90 minutes, we talked, laughed, cried, and pretended that we were on a road trip and not a rehabilitation transfer.

Arriving at Enloe Rehabilitation Center, we pulled up under the carport outside the main entrance and were greeted by a collection of aides, a nurse, and the admissions director. Their immediate presence felt somewhat intimidating and claustrophobic as they all bent down, peering into the passenger window at Judy.

With the door open, they each expressed an exuberant welcome as they introduced themselves to us. The focused attention from new and unfamiliar faces combined with her anxiety all contained within the confined space of the doorway caused Judy to break down into tears. It was too much for her to absorb in the moment. Recognizing her condition, the mini army of personnel expressed words of compassion and understanding to help ease her unsettledness.

Using the reverse process for getting Judy into the car, the team extracted her from her car seat and into the waiting wheelchair. Upon transfer completion, the team assisted in moving her through check-in and into her new home away from home, Room 105.

Enloe Rehabilitation Center was a single level, 40 bed facility with most rooms being single resident, three therapy gyms, a therapy pool, dining center, outdoor mobility court, and 24/7 care. The hallways were dotted with photos and stories of former patients who had overcome serious, traumatic injuries through the therapy provided by Enloe Rehab. The nurse's station and social services offices were located within close proximity to Judy's room. On the wall opposite the nurse's station was a large whiteboard listing all the room numbers and the schedule for each resident's various therapies for the week. It was a matrix of colors, times, numbers, and therapy abbreviations.

With a quick scouring of the board, I followed the matrix to Room 105. PT, OT, and Speech assessments were scheduled for that afternoon with full-on therapy sessions starting the next day. Judy would be undergoing, enduring, and persevering through 3-4 hours of therapy every day, Monday through Friday. Transitioning from 3-4 hours of therapy a week to that same hourly amount every day was going to be extremely intense for Judy, both mentally and physically.

The simple definition of assessment is the evaluation of the quality, ability, and developmental status of someone or something. In Judy's case, the assessment sought to determine and evaluate the severity of her deficits, the level of her cognitive skills, mental retention, vision, social interaction, hand/eye coordination, and physical capacities. In essence, the assessment evaluated every facet of her life. It was grueling and extensive with very little mercy extended. The goal was to identify Judy's best therapy course of action brutally and unapologetically.

Immediately following on the heels of her relocation and the physical toll that that took on her, the assessment drained every last ounce of endurance and stamina that Judy possessed. She gave it her all, strained every muscle she was able, followed every detailed instruction to her best ability, and so desperately wanted to not be a disappointment. She succeeded in some tests, failed in others, and struggled with many. More than once, the emotional toll was more than she could contain and she would try to hide the tears by avoiding eye contact but the water marks on the page in front of her was evidence enough.

With the assessment completed, Judy was returned to her bed and easily fell asleep from absolute exhaustion. As she napped, the therapists, head nurse, and the social worker met with me and laid out the results of their findings. They reported with blunt clarity that Judy's deficits were severe and that, while they would give every effort towards her regaining elements of what was lost, they weren't optimistic of much positive recovery and that I should begin preparing for either long term nursing home care or round the clock in-home care should she return home. The weight of their assessment landed as a fresh blow of discouraging heaviness. As they continued to talk, their words hit my ears like the voice of Charlie Brown's school teachers... unintelligible, mumbled dialogue.

At some point in the conversation, I regained a verbal connection enough to hear them explain the therapy plan of attack. It would include an hour of aggressive physical therapy twice a day, along with an hour of speech therapy and an hour of occupational therapy. Each round would push Judy to her limits with intentionality. Then came the words I wasn't expecting... "our inpatient stay is 14 days. After that, she'll need to be transferred to long term care or home."

Fourteen days! Two weeks!

In my shock, I pushed back and asked with a tone of astonishment at the thought, "Fourteen days! How is that even possible given Judy's condition? There's no way!"

"We'll begin exploring long term care options and other skilled nursing locations available with her insurance," they responded. I was starting to come to terms with the fact that insurance was going to be my new nemesis. "But we'd recommend," they continued, "that you start finding a team of people that can assist you at home and begin equipping your space to accommodate her needs."

My head was reeling from this information. The thought of Judy being moved to a third location or even home seemed beyond comprehension at this point. I couldn't imagine Judy enduring another transfer to another facility and I also couldn't grasp how life would work at home. It was all too much to fathom in the moment.

As I staggered out of the meeting, I physically and emotionally felt as if I'd been put through an extreme session of physical therapy myself. My head hurt and my body ached. Before returning to Judy's room, I needed to step outside, catch my breath, and mentally gather myself. Stepping into the fading late afternoon sunlight of the courtyard, my emotions, once again, overtook my ability to restrain them and I crumbled into a mixture of tears, anger, frustration, disappointment, and confusion. The merry-go-round of tears and emotions had become all too familiar. It was no longer cathartic.

The first evening in the dining room introduced us to a sample composition of Judy's rehab peers. The residents ranged in age and degrees of need. Of the 20 individuals dotted around the various tables, the majority were older than Judy and appeared to be recovering from falls, hip replacements, and heart surgeries. Most were physically mobile and agile enough to feed themselves and enjoy a regular array of edible food. A few joined with others and carried on conversations as they ate but most sat at tables by themselves. Judy didn't want or have the energy to converse and so we found a table against the wall where we could be by ourselves. With Judy's wheelchair securely positioned at the table, an aide approached us, introduced herself and placed an adult bib over Judy's head.

Even though Judy was many years younger than her dining counterparts, her condition was noticeably more severe. Since she was sitting up at a table, she required a neck pillow to keep her head centered and upright. She required a SafeStraw for drinking liquids. A SafeStraw provides a limited swallowable amount of liquid by use of a fluid chamber, one way valve, and a float. As Judy sucked on the straw, the liquid flowed through the valve and into the chamber, causing the float to rise. As the float rose, it only allowed enough for Judy to swallow without aspirating. Given her left side deficit and inability to fully navigate an eating utensil to her mouth and regulate the amount of food in each bite with her right hand, she required an aide to sit with her through her entire meal to assist her. It was essential that Judy only ingest a minimal amount of food in each bite. Therefore, her diet would be sparse, repetitive, and guarded.

As I watched Judy open her mouth on cue to receive each bite of her spoon-fed meal, the cinematic mix-reel in my mind started replaying scenes from what seemed like a distant galaxy far, far away…

…the evening of our first anniversary when our bank account was limited but our love was overflowing and so we turned our little upstairs apartment with its slanted floors and opposite slanted ceiling into an Italian osteria with candles, cheap wine, and the single item in the menu being spaghetti.

…her indefatigable attempts to expand my vegetable palate beyond corn, iceberg lettuce, and the occasional green bean. These were attempts in futility but she was persistent.

…her ability to throw together whatever we had in the cupboards and make a meal. Sometimes the quality of the experimental mixture was below her expectations, but she gave it her all and we ate it anyway.

…the thrill of victory and the agony of defeat as a mom when it came to the struggle of getting our kids to eat, incorporating all the tried-and-true tactics of the train coming around the mountain, the plane coming in for a landing, and the hungry dinosaur ready for a big bite. Sometimes it worked with ease, other times more food ended up on the floor than in their mouths. We took the wins when we could.

It may be starting to sound redundant or, at least, redundant in my own mind but as I saw Judy in her current quality of life, I saw how fragile and broken her body was. She wasn't a machine or an AI robot where parts could be inserted and replaced with mechanical ease and a little tweaking and all would be good again. Judy was a human being that needed healing. Her brokenness was not evidence that her faith wasn't strong enough, or that God wasn't near enough, or that God didn't care enough. Her brokenness, displayed with every assisted small bite of food, was evidence of how desperate we are to remain close to the God who created us. We are not masters of our own destiny.

Too often we're slaves to our own emotions and our own circumstances. Too often we're slaves to what society or our upbringing forces upon us. We take on an orphan mentality which, in turn, leaves us reactionary rather than proactive. Our behavior and thinking react and are conditional upon who's around us and what's happening, leaving us feeling insecure and that love must be earned. We hide. We pretend. We end up responding from an orphaned state of mind with its restrictions, confinements, insecurities, and fears rather than living in the freedom of our fullest identity in Christ.

But when we're moving towards despair in the whirlwind of circumstances beyond our control, it seems like the crisis that we're facing is permanent. It feels like the crisis will never end. That this is the way it will always be. The voices in our heads start declaring that this worst moment, that this traumatic, dark intrusion now defines our future. This is it!

But it's not the truth. Even if the darkness and trauma and crisis don't necessarily dissipate, none of those things, not even our brokenness, get to define us or our future. As my mental cinematic replay was ending at this dining room table and as I considered this gift of life in front of me being spoon-fed, it struck me afresh that Judy's brokenness was undeniable but it did not define her identity which had been established before time began and would carry her forward.

Returning Judy to her room that evening, it was very apparent that she was thoroughly exhausted and ready for bed. The arduous ordeal of her day had drained every ounce of energy, composure, and strength that she contained. But getting her to bed would not happen quickly. Being understaffed and overworked, the few CNAs were on constant call from the residents, all in crisis and, in their minds, needing immediate assistance. This meant that Judy's transfer from her wheelchair to her bed fell further down the list of priorities. So, we waited. And waited. And waited some more. Every waiting moment increased Judy's level of physical uncomfortableness, the need for hygiene attention, and her desire for sleep. Every waiting moment also increased my frustration and my exasperated visits to the nurse's station requesting help were to no avail. Finally, after almost two hours of waiting, at 8:00pm, Judy was transferred to her bed, cleaned, changed, and ready to sleep but far from calm.

I was frustrated, angry, and disturbed. The day had been unbelievably long for both Judy and I and the ending only made it maddeningly longer. While I rationally understood that it wasn't the CNAs' fault, the circumstances were unacceptable.

"I don't want you to go. Don't go. I don't want you to leave me alone here," Judy pleaded as I indicated that the hour was late, and I needed to go. I had no other choice as COVID protocols didn't allow me to stay overnight nor was there extra space in her room to do so even if staying was an option. She reached out her hand to me, which I quickly grasped in mine, and she began to sob with soundless wails. I attempted to reassure Judy that she was going to be alright and with Thanksgiving in two days, I promised her that I would be back in time to meet her for breakfast that morning and we'd spend the day together. Thanksgiving in rehab was not what we had hoped but we'd do it, as we had done the previous 36 years, with each other.

My words did little to assuage her trepidation in the moment. Squeezing her hand one more time, I expressed how much I loved her and left the room. As I walked down the long hallway to the exit, the emotional gamut swirled through my head. If I could have changed places with Judy, I would have in a heartbeat. Even though it had been 82 consecutive nights of leaving her in a bed not her own at home, it wasn't getting any easier. If anything, it was getting harder. Not only harder leaving her but also harder facing my own aloneness.

For 36 years, her breathing next to me at night was my white noise that soothed me to sleep. For all those nights, her presence was my joy when times were good and my comfort when times were difficult. Many a night, her arms around me held me together and gave me strength. In recalling that, I hope that I've reciprocated in the same way for Judy over that same length of life. Now, for 82 nights, I'd been alone and in that span of time I've learned the significant distinction between loneliness and aloneness.

I was certainly not lonely. I had a supportive community around me which included my family and dear, dear friends. A small contingent of people who regularly checked in with me and made sure I was eating and functioning in a somewhat reasonably healthy fashion. So, I wasn't lonely.

But I was alone.

There was an unavoidable solitude that came with something this life altering. It still came down to only me and Jesus when I was lying in bed at night. And it was in those night hours that the mind could just…run. Every thought, every situation, every decision, every imagined circumstance raced through my mind like a thundering freight train in the empty darkness. All of which had the potential to create so much anxiety. But the feeling of aloneness would overtake me in those hours. It's what I felt when I felt untethered to reality. It's what I felt when the thought of making one more decision seemed overwhelming. It's what I felt when I couldn't stand the silence. It's what I felt when I sensed no one could identify with what Judy and I were enduring. It's what I felt when faced with the possibility of Judy not recovering. It's what I felt when I felt vulnerable, and that life and I were a disappointment.

The world felt so big and I seemed so small and irrelevant. With so many worldwide crises occurring, Judy and I's personal trauma seemed so inconsequential to the vast landscape of humanity at the time. It was just Judy and I and I was alone. But I couldn't allow that to be the final period of the story. I had to preach to myself. I needed to exhort my own soul that while the world felt so big and I felt so small, the God who made me and lived within me was so big. Even though I was irrelevant to the world, I was relevant and known by God. I recall that it was in one of those reminder moments that God broke into my thought process and asked, "What do you need?"

"God, I need Judy healed. That's on You. I need you to work out this nightmare with all the decisions. God, I need you to get Judy home."

My prayers were becoming much more blunt and direct.

"No," God responded, "what do YOU need?"

In that question-and-answer moment with God, this verse came to my mind, "I (Jesus) have told you all this so that you may have peace in me. Here on earth you will have many trials and sorrows. But take heart, because I have overcome the world (John 16:33 NLT).

Before I could answer I sensed God interject, "Son, you've got all you need. I'm in this with you. I've got this. Take heart, Judy is mine. Whether healing happens or not, I've got her."

With Judy being only 90 minutes south of home, one of her few requests from me was that I would arrive in time for breakfast on the days that I visited. That request became my absolute priority. Knowing she'd be watching for me, I made sure to be at her table by 8:00am. Upon seeing me walk into the dining room, Judy would burst into tears and upon seeing her beautiful face, I would do the same. We were a mess and I'm sure a sight to behold by the others in the room eating their eggs and oatmeal. My new weekly rhythm had me with Judy on Monday,

Wednesday, and Saturday and working full time at my day job as staff at the church on Tuesday, Thursday, Friday and all-day Sunday. It was exhausting but necessary. This was life with no other breathing space. If possible, I would attempt to surprise Judy on an occasional weeknight as a bonus visit. No matter when I arrived, our reunions were special.

Days spent with Judy were far from a day off or relaxing for me. As soon as breakfast was satisfactorily completed, therapy would begin. Judy was repositioned from the dining room to the gym where she was met, usually, by a trio of physical therapists. Eager and enthusiastic, the three amigas would waste little time in maneuvering Judy from her wheelchair and onto the exercise bed, a standing frame, or the MOTOmed. Each location, piece of equipment, and exercise was strategically selected with Judy's deficits and recovery in mind. The primary goal was to get her brain engaged in activating her motor skills and muscle movement. Whether it was working her core, having her stand for extended periods of time, pedal, reach, push, or pull, it was a full 60 minutes of intense, ruthless hard labor as it needed to be. The gift in it all was that while the therapists offered no mercy and allowed for little rest, they were full of compassion and empathy for Judy, offering loads of encouragement and motivation. To no surprise, Judy quickly became a favorite among the therapists.

Following physical therapy, Judy was returned to her bed for a brief nap and a time to recover. It didn't last long, however, as speech therapy was soon on the clock. Of the three therapies: physical, occupational, and speech, speech therapy was the most difficult, emotionally draining, and repeatedly disheartening for Judy. Judy loved math, word usage, and vocabulary. She had excelled at reading comprehension and visual identification. Words were powerful and important to her and she offered them with thought and care. Now, with her wheelchair squeezed into the speech therapist's small office filled with certifications on the wall, shelves of therapeutic textbooks, notebooks of speech therapy exercise suggestions, and a desk organized with neatly stacked files and papers, Judy sat struggling to comply with simple swallowing instructions, decipher addition and subtraction problems, and identify missing items on matching pictures.

I'm not sure if the speech therapist was intentionally trying to be intimidating as a motivational tactic or if it was purely her character but whichever the case, her demeanor and intensity were stifling for Judy. As the therapist pressed Judy for answers or reasons for why she couldn't complete the task in front of her or follow the verbal instructions, I could see Judy withdrawing, wishing she could escape from the room. Again, inaudible sobs would begin, and all she could muster was, "I don't know." But with "still a lot of fight" left in her, I would see Judy, in her next breath, lean in, set her focus on the exercise, and try again. She wasn't going to give up. The problem wasn't going to get the best of her. I was so proud of her determination even if the correct answer or the completed exercise still eluded her in the end.

After lunch, followed round three of therapy: Occupational therapy. Occupational therapists directed their attention on Judy being able to recover skills that were necessary for everyday life. The end goal was to be able to equip Judy with the ability to manage small tasks in the kitchen, assist with her self-care, and re-establish a semblance of normalcy to her life. But before any of that could happen, it was necessary for Judy to regain some brain/muscle connection and coordination with her left arm and hand. As the days continued to pass post-stroke, the likelihood of Judy experiencing an optimistic recovery was diminishing. The 60-90 day window that stroke recovery experts give for the optimum chance for the neuroplasticity of the brain to redirect and rewire connections with Judy's deficits had closed. Recovery was less likely. But Judy and I believed that words such as, "less likely," "improbable" and "impossible" were the onramps for God to the miraculous.

At each OT session, the therapist would attach an E-Stim device on Judy's left wrist and forearm. E-Stim stands for electrical stimulation. Electrical stimulation works by placing noninvasive electrodes on the patient's skin. Once the device is turned on, these electrodes send mild electrical impulses to the affected muscles, causing them to contract and move. In stroke recovery this can help engage the damaged portions of the brain and, in a sense, trick the brain into reconnecting with muscle movement. When the therapist activated the device, she'd instruct Judy to pull her left arm towards her body across the table. With the electrical stimulation and light assistance from the therapist, Judy would strain to engage her muscles and put her arm in motion. Movement would happen in short spurts making it difficult to determine how much the electrical stimulation, therapist assistance, or Judy's brain was actually creating the response. Any movement, no matter how slight and regardless of the cause behind it, was a brief moment of encouragement. Even if the movement was barely perceptible or more psychological than real, it ignited a rekindling of hope.

At Enloe Rehab Center, it became very apparent that Judy needed incremental steps of present moment hope rather than big picture, future possibilities. Her spirit was hungry for small steps in a forward direction. Realizing this placed me in the tension of needing to wear interchangeable hats between spouse and cheerleader. At times, it was difficult to know which hat was needed more or would be the most helpful in the moment. I would support and comfort one moment and then applaud and encourage the next. The palpable tension within me was that I so deeply wanted to protect and shield Judy from any more disappointment or struggle while also wanting her to put in every ounce of effort towards recovery. I wanted to protect; recovery was calling her to perform. I wanted to shelter her; recovery wanted her to sweat. I wanted to pause; recovery wanted to press. It was in those moments that I, again, found myself wishing that I could switch places with Judy and have it be me that was being called to perform, sweat, and press. If possible, I would have switched places without a second thought.

The insurance quagmire was becoming a nightmare. I admit

that I was naïve, in so many ways, when it came to the health insurance world. Maybe not so much naïve as adopting the motto that "ignorance was bliss." Judy and I had previously worked through the circus of finding an acceptable and affordable marketplace health insurance plan. Being viewed as "self-employed" by the IRS as a minister and not having health insurance provided by either of our employers, we had to find our own policy with all its limitations and regulations. It required us to continually watch our household income percentage in comparison to the federal poverty level. Too much annual income and we were hit with a massive insurance repayment tax. So, it forced us to forego annual bonuses or raises if it would push us over the income ceiling. Or, we had to get intentional with investing in our IRA's to reduce our reported income level. But, while this caused a high level of angst in me as the end of the year always approached, at least we had health insurance.

The current quagmire was due to the fact that while we had health insurance, our health insurance provider wasn't accepted by the majority of long-term care facilities. A second facet of our quagmire was that Judy was too young to qualify for Medicare, being that she was only 61 with age eligibility needing to be 65. A third facet was that I earned too much, which was hard to fathom as a minister, for us to qualify for Medi-Cal as California residents. So that further restricted long-term care facility options.

December 14th marked the two-week deadline imposed by Enloe Rehab for Judy's stay. Each day that I was present, I had a meeting with the social workers overseeing Judy's case to receive an update on any progress, usually the lack thereof, related to long-term facility options. While the social worker team was honestly trying their best to match our insurance with any potential facilities within our geographical area, the reality is that none were available, and our home wasn't set up to handle Judy's needs which prevented coming home as a viable alternative. The stress of Judy's physical situation, the stress of needing to be her constant advocate, the stress of needing to maintain a semblance of presence and responsibility at work, the stress of holding daily life together, all combined with the stress and pressure of needing to figure out the next piece of Judy's facility puzzle was becoming more than I could handle. I wasn't sleeping well. I wasn't eating well. My nervous system felt in disarray. I felt out of sync and out of sorts and yet I felt the internalized pressure to give the appearance of having it all together. More than all of that, I felt like I was disappointing Judy, my kids, my work team, everyone. My emotions were high. Any slight inconvenience, expectation, or emotional trigger would set me off with either anger or tears or discouragement or all three. I sensed, more than ever, that I was tipping into despair. I remember reading that when one life partner suffers a brain injury, the other partner does as well. Judy wasn't the only one who suffered a brain injury, so did I. Although very different in degrees and nature, we'd both been hit with mental and physical trauma.

When anyone would inquire about Judy's condition, I very rarely was able to hold it together emotionally. I was tired of crying. I wanted to yell! I wanted to not have to answer! I wanted to escape! I wanted to run! I wanted my tribe of people around me, and I wanted to be left alone. Trauma was leading me to isolation. What I've since discovered is that traumatized fear, isolation, and stress result in dampened cognitive function. Memory capacity, rational calculation and quick thinking all become diminished because the trauma has created neurochemical chaos in the brain. That chaos sent me into survival mode wherein I felt I was incapable any longer of accessing or processing critical intel in order to make sound decisions. Trauma was diluting discernment. Everything was coming at me at a speed that I was unable keep up with. Normal life allows for mindful space, trauma eliminates it. Yet, I couldn't quit. Judy wasn't giving up so neither was I.

December 14th came and went. No facility changes. In the meantime, the good news was that Judy was able to continue with her daily routine of therapy sessions. As long as she was in rehab, she received therapy. At the same time, the pressure was mounting for me to adapt our home to accommodate Judy's physical needs. The idea of Judy coming home was becoming our only option. Another week went by, still nothing. Our insurance provider notified Enloe Rehab that they were discontinuing coverage of Judy's expenses due to the lack of noticeable improvement in her condition per the doctor's report. It was only because of the lack of being able to confirm Judy's safety at home that kept her from being heartlessly and automatically discharged from rehab. I made it a point to keep Judy out of these discussions and clear of the pressing circumstances. She had enough to think about and focus on. This was my burden to carry for her sake.

The reality of celebrating Christmas in rehab in Chico was surreal and discouraging. We both longed for and anticipated being home by Christmas. Three months earlier, Christmas was outlined as our target date to be home and well on the road to recovery. We had our hearts set on being in our own cozy confines, surrounded with the aroma of pine from our tree, the glow of the lights, the heartwarming familiarity of our decorations, and the joy of opening gifts. Instead, the house was mostly void of Christmas decorations except for a few displayed by some dear friends in a kind attempt to make our space festive. But no tree, no lights, and little evidence of holiday joy. While all that was true, I wouldn't allow "humbug" to define this Christmas, however. So much had already been taken from us, I wasn't going to allow Christmas to be fully absorbed into the loss column as well.

On Christmas morning, I packed all our gifts to each other (I bought my own for myself with her in mind and wrapped them) in two suitcases and delivered them to Judy's room. After breakfast and with Judy having been returned to bed, we joyfully opened our presents one at a time. Even though her left side deficit hindered Judy from opening her presents on her own, we didn't give those deficits much space to be acknowledged. Not on this day. This was a day to celebrate. Her smile, though still crooked, was so cheerful as she relished the moment. Because it was Christmas, no therapy was on the calendar. We had the entire day to ourselves. Judy was able to rest, watch her Hallmark Christmas movies for as long as she could endure them, take naps, FaceTime our kids, and take a leisurely afternoon excursion to the outside patio. I, on the other hand, thankfully received uninterrupted hours to be with her. It was the perfect gift for me.

Before the cherished hours of the day concluded, I opened Judy's Bible and read aloud the beautiful words of the nativity story and the wonder of Jesus' birth. In the imperfect and otherworldly circumstances that we found ourselves in this Christmas, it made the birth of our Savior into this imperfect and otherworldly environment of humanity that much more impactful and personal. While Judy and I did not willfully or purposefully enter into our world of chaos, Jesus, on the other hand, "gave up his divine privileges, he took the humble position of a slave and was born as a human being" (Philippians 2:7 NLT). The remarkable wonder is that God, at just the right time, "sent his Son, born of a woman, subject to the law. God sent him to buy freedom for us who were slaves to the law, so that he could adopt us as his very own children" (Galatians 4:4-5 NLT). Jesus willfully and purposefully left the splendor of heaven to step into our mess entirely FOR us. In our broken condition, Jesus met us. As Judy and I clung to the last remaining moments of that sacred space, she asked to sing her favorite Christmas carols. So, we did. With voices cracking from emotion, slurred speech, and imperfect pitch, we sang. It wasn't perfect but it was beautiful. The room reverberated with the sounds of Advent. As I quieted my voice to hear hers, I marveled at this gift of life in front of me. Her body damaged, exhausted, and nowhere near where she wanted to be, yet her heart was full of hope and joy.

The New Year offered no reprieve from the stroke's toll on

Judy's body and the days continued to add up in our never-ending unproductive quest for a long-term care facility. As much as I wanted to ignore the signs, the reality was that Judy's physical disabilities were not improving at an acceptable pace. In fact, the word "plateaued" was being verbalized with more regularity. In Judy's condition, this was not a good assessment.

* * *

On January 8, 2022, Judy was admitted to the Enloe Medical Center. When visiting with her the day before, it was apparent that she seemed "off." She was more disoriented and thirstier than normal which, having been around this block several times before, was indicative of her sodium level being out of whack. In bringing it to the Rehab staff's attention, they dismissed her status as due to being tired and nothing to be concerned about. That was not an acceptable response. I knew better. Having become accustomed to fiercely being Judy's advocate, I aggressively persuaded the CNAs to check her vitals. As I expected with frustration, her sodium level was extremely high and so she was admitted to the Medical Center for treatment and observation. While waiting for the transfer from Enloe Rehab to Enloe Medical Center to occur, I was advised to pack up all of Judy's items from her room. All her clothing, décor, personal items, medications, paperwork...everything had to be packed. And it was necessary that it all be packed and out of her room by the time we left. Not being forewarned that this was on the agenda, I had no suitcases or travel bags with me to carry out such an immediate endeavor. So, the staff provided garbage bags for me to stuff everything into. No time to fold or organize, it all just needed to get into the bags and out to my car. The rush and absurdity of the timing felt extremely odd and so I inquired as to why it had to happen at that moment. The response presented to me was that if Judy required hospitalization for more than a few days, there could be the possibility that her room would need to be given to a potential new resident. The charge nurse continued by reassuring me that while the likelihood of such an event happening was rare, Judy would, no matter what, be guaranteed a room upon her hospital discharge.

While the disruption with Judy's accommodations was unsettling, I was more concerned with her physical condition. Here we were, once again, in a hospital. Our third hospital in four months. Even though each hospital was in a different region of northern California, they all contained unavoidable similarities. Similar smells, alarms and codes, personnel in their colored scrubs identifying their medical roles, levels of heightened activity, the hope for healing, and the reality of death. This particular hospital excursion called for Judy to stay a week until her sodium returned to an acceptable level. It's unbelievable how routine her sodium imbalances had become that I only give it one sentence at this point in her story. What was so unnerving a few months before was now becoming commonplace in the new rhythm of our lives. Unfortunately, sodium imbalance would be a constant, intrusive, and unwanted companion on Judy's journey.

Three days into Judy's current hospitalization, however, I was summoned to a meeting with the hospital social worker. Impromptu meetings such as this were jarring to my nervous system as I, almost reflexively, had become conditioned to assume the worst. The social worker proceeded to inform me that Judy's room at Enloe Rehab had, indeed, been given to another resident and no other rooms were available. The "guarantee" of a space for her was non-existent. The news that Judy was unable to return was beyond disappointing and frustrating. It felt hurtful and personal. My cynical side made the determination that the rehab social workers conceived of this plan upon hearing of Judy needing to be hospitalized. It was a convenient way of offloading Judy and her facility-finding struggle from their collective conscience and why it was so urgent for me to pack up all her belongings before she left. They, I deduced, knew that Judy wouldn't be returning. Again, that was my cynical side at work. I have no idea if that was their hastily concocted plan.

As I, once again, traversed hospital hallways with a clouded sense of confusion and disbelief, I had a choice to make. I could either emotionally spin over the maddening circumstances presented to us or I could step into action and develop a plan. Judy needed me to create a plan for her. Sitting and spiraling wasn't going to resolve her primary need for a place to go upon discharge in a few days. So, setting my emotional upheaval aside, I formulated Judy's next step. She was coming HOME!

PART IV

Home

The Enloe Medical Center social worker indicated that she could resume the search for a long-term care facility or a suitable nursing home for Judy, but I determined that we were done exploring that route. One nursing home had risen as a possibility but it was south of Sacramento which would have put Judy over three hours away from home and that wasn't acceptable. I couldn't fathom my Judy being isolated in a nursing home at a location further away than ever and me returning to the horrendous routine of only being able to see her for a few hours at a time, a few days a week due to travel. But more than the strain that would put on me, I recognized the unbearable strain it would put on Judy. I believed that the separation, loneliness, isolation, and the confines of that environment would have been traumatizing and sent her into unrecoverable despair. I couldn't do that to her. When it's the center of your world who is lying in a bed and you see the toll that's taking place in the journey, I knew it was time for her to come home.

With the decision made, I had to shift my entire mindset into "go mode" for Judy's homecoming. My administrative gifting and skillset went into high gear. I knew this would be, without a doubt, the most challenging undertaking of my life. I had no idea if I was up to the task, but I knew without question that it was the right course of action. Step one was that I needed to make an immediate transition of our home space into a safe place for Judy to live. That required me to acquire a list of necessities to make her life comfortable and functional. Those necessities included a hospital bed, a manual Hoyer Lift, a bedside commode, portable shower bench, a wheelchair, therapy equipment, a closet full of personal hygiene items, and a mountain sized amount of adult briefs.

Thankfully I had a team that rallied to my aid. I'm so grateful for their compassion and help. I share this as a testament to God's faithfulness and the power of community. A loving team from our church rearranged the furniture to make our bedroom and living room more wheelchair and handicap friendly. They reconfigured our kitchen so that items were more accessible for Judy at a wheelchair height. This team arranged and stocked our hygiene closet and gifted us with a power lift recliner. That recliner would prove to be a Godsend for Judy. A friend who worked for a medical equipment company got all our equipment needs generously donated, delivered, and set up for us. Family members gifted us with exercise items, other handicap assist accessories, and a recurring paid subscription order for diapers. It's important to say that all of this happened within a span of 4 days. It was truly miraculous, and I was, and still am, overwhelmed by the generosity and compassion expressed by all involved. It wouldn't have been possible to get Judy home without them.

Early on in our poststroke journey, I made a personal and unwavering commitment to provide Judy with the best of what she needed. If it was necessary for her to enjoy life, be comfortable, and cared for, she wasn't going to receive second best. That commitment clearly extended itself to what we needed at home. I researched everything, to the best of my ability, from the best skin sensitive bath products to the most helpful wound care aids to the top home therapy equipment like what Judy had in rehab to the most comfortable mattress to the best protective bed railing to the easiest eating utensils for stroke survivors. I researched everything and even though there may have been less expensive items on the market, I wanted Judy to have the best that I could provide for her. I needed her to feel absolutely and unquestionably cared for. Maybe this said more about me and my mental state than hers.

I needed Judy to feel cared for.

I needed Judy to be comfortable.

I needed Judy to know she was loved and valued.

I needed Judy to feel safe.

I needed Judy to know that I was doing my best.

I needed to know that I was of use.

I needed to know that while often over the past four months feeling like I couldn't do a damn thing to help, I was helping now.

I needed to know that it wasn't my fault.

Survivor's guilt had been introduced into my vocabulary and psyche without invitation, and I don't attach that response to the trauma I experienced frivolously. The most common response to survivor's guilt is feeling responsible for what happened, repeatedly asking myself what I could have done differently to possibly change the now real outcome. "If only I…" is the unfinished statement that unrelentingly keeps running through my mind. Added to that are thoughts of not having done enough, not responding fast enough, and not making the correct decisions.

"If only I had acted sooner, responded differently to Judy's symptoms the day before, or had not given her space to take a nap that Saturday afternoon, maybe I could have prevented this from happening to Judy. If only I had chosen a different hospital or a different rehab facility, Judy wouldn't be in this condition. It's my fault. Judy would have done it better and differently."

Survivor's guilt has been described as having a form of PTSD with an added layer of guilt and what's sinister about it is that while I rationally know that these "If only I…" statements are untethered to reality, they carry profound weight that feels very real. The result is that I feel responsible to make up for the deficits inflicted upon Judy.

Our place now readied for Judy's homecoming and with her sodium back within a healthier range, discharge from Enloe Medical Center was scheduled for January 14, 2022. Discharge was smooth, the transfer from the hospital chair to the car was rough, but the ride home was a joyous, tearful celebration. Even though I-5 was a very familiar road to Judy with landmarks that had long ago lost their interest and excitement, those same landmarks were, on this day, poignant indicators of our increasing nearness to home. Accompanying frequent stretches of miles, Judy's emotions would flow. While she was unable to fully express the emotions she was experiencing, I believe it was a mixture of happiness and trepidation. Relief in coming home and reservation in the unknown. The closer we got to home, the more anxious she became.

We pulled into our driveway, and I put our car in Park. Our days of separation were over. Leaning towards Judy, I exclaimed, "We're home!" expecting her enthusiasm to match mine. But it didn't. Again, with tears flowing, she said, "I'm afraid to get out." Assuming she was referring to her insecurity about my ability to physically transfer her from the car to the wheelchair and getting her inside, I reassured her that it was going to be great and that there was no way that I was going to let anything happen to her. I wasn't going to drop her. But that wasn't it. "I'm afraid to get out," she repeated. "I don't want to go in."

That's when it struck me. The last time Judy left our home was in a panic-induced state of trauma. Her last recollection of home was fear, shock, and being hastily wheeled to the car, unable to move or barely speak. A lifetime of change had occurred since then. While Judy and I were overjoyed at the thought of her coming home, we weren't psychologically and emotionally prepared for the home she was coming back to not being the same home she left 133 days ago.

Judy's homecoming involved radical adjustments. She came home to a house that was now outfitted for a disabled individual. She came home to rooms occupied with medical equipment and handicapped accessible elements. As appreciative and grateful as we were for the necessary equipment to help Judy function and provide some mobility and comfort, they were all every-moment reminders that her home was different.

In August 2021, she could walk in the door with ease.

In January 2022, she had to be wheeled in.

In August 2021, she maneuvered through our home without limitation.

In January 2022, she was faced with everything being a limitation.

In August 2021, she viewed our home as a representation of optimism and peace.

In January 2022, she viewed our home as a representation of loss and unsettledness.

In August 2021, her home was a place filled with a memorable past.

In January 2022, her home was a place filled with an unknown future.

Home was radically different. Not only for Judy but for me as well.

My first official task, after introducing Judy to her home again and positioning her in the recliner for its inaugural recline, was to make dinner. I had made dinner for Judy countless times over our married years but never like that one. That dinner carried significance, weightiness, and the changing of seasons for us. With that meal, I stepped into what would become my most precious and honored role in my life…Judy's care giver. I was certainly not prepared for the avalanche of duties that would cascade upon me as I lifted each spoonful to her mouth that evening, but I was determined to do everything within my power and strength to make sure Judy's needs were met and that she was taken care of.

Through moments of weeping conveying relief and angst, celebration and grief in the precious hours of that night, I caught Judy with a pensive expression. In asking her what she was thinking, Judy paused for a second to form her thoughts and said, "I've ruined your life. You'll never have a good day again." Hearing those words broke my heart. That was her assessment of my current plight. I knew that it was the emotion of the day motivating those thoughts but they hit me with such sorrow. I hurriedly knelt beside her and encouraged her to look me in the eyes, "Judy, you're home. It's the best day of my life, outside of the day I married you. We'll take every day as it comes. We'll be fine. But you're going to have to put in the work with me. You're home and I'm here with you."

Reflecting on the day's events after Judy had fallen asleep, my mind recalled Jesus' story in Luke 15 about the lost son or the "prodigal son" as he is more familiarly labeled as. In the story, Jesus identifies the youngest son as the rebellious one who goes against the cultural grain by asking for his inheritance before his father has passed away. The son's request was incredibly culturally inappropriate. But what's more incredible is that, in the story, the father does exactly what the younger son asks for. The father gives the son his inheritance. But adding even more to the incredibleness is that the father gives the son his inheritance even though he knows his son is going to blow it all. Which is exactly how the story played out.

The younger son greedily takes the money and runs. He goes to a distant land and squanders everything he has, leaving him penniless and living in the muck and mire with a herd of pigs. His life has come to a complete stop. What that tells me is that leaving home is easy when you want to run away.

It's easy to leave.

It's easy to walk out the door when my narcissistic radar is fixed on me.

It's easy to leave for the proverbial distant land when the only thing that matters is my quest for freedom.

The son had freedom, land, and a home with his father. He had everything he needed. Yet he chose a distant land, a land of his own choosing, a land outside of the grace and love of his father as his place of residence. I wonder how many "prodigal sons" we know who talked all about wanting to be free and experience life within the margins they defined but when it came down to reality, the weight of freedom was more than they could carry. The responsibility of freedom and living life their way was more than they could manage. They wanted to live it up before they had grown up.

In the story that Jesus is telling, the son ends up stuck. He's not in the land he imagined he'd be in and he's not home. He's in between. The son's not in the bright lights of the big city and he's not home, he's in between in a field. After some self-reflection, the son decides that it's better that he return home than stay in squalor with the pigs. The decision wasn't easy for the son, but it was the best decision. Coming home was the right choice even though he had no comprehension of what home would be. What he encountered was love, acceptance, and hope.

Though vastly different circumstances for the prodigal son and for Judy, coming home for both was the most difficult undertaking of their lives but it was also the most necessary. Home is where our deepest sense of belonging resides. Home is where starting over shouldn't be an obstacle but an opportunity. Yes, coming home can be difficult but it should be where hope lives.

With Judy now home, there was an understandable increasing pressure to resume more of a full-time presence at work. My team had been gracious in allowing such flexibility in my schedule and absences while Judy was in rehab but that couldn't continue. The demands of a growing staff and a vibrantly active large church called for me to be hands-on again. But because Judy was unable to be left alone, it meant that I needed to hire or recruit home care to fill in the daily time slots when I couldn't be there. Once again, however, we found ourselves in the unenviable gap between our standard of living and the availability of social services assistance. Repeating the same disqualifications of making an income above the poverty level, Judy's age, and our "wrong" insurance, we were denied daily home care assistance. Any help that Judy would require would need to come from out-of-pocket. The system felt broken, unhelpful, and so unsympathetic. Both Judy and I had been hard working employees our entire adult lives. We paid our taxes. We were law abiding citizens. We paid our health insurance premiums. We loved our neighbors and valued the communities we lived in. Yet, in our time of unexpected need, the repeated answer I received was, "No, you do not qualify."

In voicing my frustration over our predicament, the options presented to me were even more incredulous. One option seriously voiced to me was since my income was "too much" and we filed taxes jointly, I could divorce Judy as a benefit to her. She would then not be included in my income and since she then wouldn't have any income, she would qualify for all the state's health services. I could still live with her, but we'd technically be divorced. Unbelievable!

A second "viable" option was to acquire a second living location that would be identified as my primary residence. The reasoning behind this suggestion was that since, on paper, I wouldn't be living with Judy full-time, even though I was her husband, she would receive health care benefits because she didn't have a full-time partner to watch over her. Again, unbelievable!

In some ways, I understood the drastic measures offered to me as possible options. They were "do whatever is necessary to make it work" possibilities but both of those options were off the table. Even though the system felt broken, I wasn't going to work the system in ways that violated my values. Therefore, I had to make it work myself.

Recruiting a small army of volunteers to sit with Judy was no small task. Several wonderful friends each committed to spending a few hours a week with her. No care giving was required but their presence and encouragement to Judy was invaluable. Also, God miraculously blessed us with two licensed CNA's who, for an interim, were available to stay with Judy two days a week. Rachel and Brittney were Godsends. Under their individual watches of time, I was able to go about my responsibilities with the peace of mind that Judy was taken care of but if anything did arise, Rachel and Brittney knew what to do. In the ongoing whirlwind of life, these gifts of help were respites in the storm.

Judy's daily routine became established fairly quickly once she arrived home. Due to the need for assistance in every aspect of her life, our mornings started early. First things first, with her continuing incontinence it called for me to get her cleaned and changed. Learning to do this with gentleness while maintaining dignity for Judy was paramount for me. Needing to do this for her several times throughout the day became an honored act of service. The inconvenience she had to endure was my invitation to love. Next came the often-humorous process of getting her dressed. Without the ability for her to sit up on her own or navigate her left arm and leg through sleeves and pants created some strategic obstacles for us but we always persevered. Without fail, every time I maneuvered the neck opening from her shirt over her head and her face reappeared, she would give me the sweetest smile. It was her way of celebrating our victorious accomplishment.

The responsibility to transfer Judy from any and every location rested on me. Success or failure was thoroughly dependent on her body positioning, wheelchair placement, and the initial surge of momentum. With those elements in place, the "stand/pivot" maneuver would happen seamlessly. However, each "what" to "where" contained their individual challenges. Transferring Judy from her bed to the wheelchair required a different strategy compared to transferring her from her wheel-chair to the recliner and transferring her from the wheelchair to the car seat was a whole different ball game. With repetition, though, each transfer became more and more routine. My best friend in most transferring endeavors was the manual Hoyer Lift. The "Hoyer" was a lifesaver. This piece of equipment protected my back from overstraining and gently moved Judy from her recliner and back into her bed or from her recliner into her wheelchair with ease. The individual who invented this machine was a genius.

Our daily routine included Judy's favorite breakfast foods, listening to the audible Bible, attempts at regular home therapy exercises, watching her beloved Netflix shows, lunch, afternoon nap, visiting friends and games of UNO, supper together with the Andy Griffith Show, and bedtime. This was quite the different rhythm of her days compared to the independent, ener-getic, full-time working Judy that I had known for so many years. So much had been taken away from her, yet she continued to seek out purpose for each day. One beautiful intentional aspect of that purpose-seeking desire of her heart was to end each day listening to worship music as she fell asleep. The calming and encouraging presence of God created through the lyrics and melodies of our dear friends, Dan and Sandy, old hymns, and other familiar songs soothed her mind as she drifted to sleep. As much as she was able and for as long as she could stay awake, Judy would close her eyes and attempt to join in the chorus of praise to Jesus, whom she so dearly loved.

Judy, for as long as I had known her, longed to be a singer. She loved to sing and had the ability to stay on pitch, carry a tune, and harmonize quite beautifully. Along with her sisters and mom, she had grown up providing Sunday morning musical specials in their Methodist Church. After encountering the power of life change through Jesus later in life, Judy took advan-tage of every opportunity to lift her voice in praise. It was truly her heart's desire. While her voice wasn't "America's Got Talent" worthy, it was beautiful enough, I guarantee, to catch the ear of heaven. Which made the loss of her ability to carry a tune, stay on time with the music's cadence, and remember the lyrics such a cruel consequence of the stroke's impact on her brain. The stroke had tried to mercilessly squelch her song but to no avail. With breathy and limited vocal power, unrhythmic tune, and sporadic words, Judy would softly sing her praise as if Jesus was her only audience while the tears rolled down her cheeks and the day drew to a close. It was wholly beautiful for me to witness and holy sacred for me to hear. Being in the room as her voice carried her worship was hallowed ground.

Shortly after Judy's homecoming, our kids traveled from their extended locations to visit. That was our first, in person, family gathering since the early days of Judy's stroke and hospitalization. This was also their first full exposure to Judy in her current condition. I can't fully comprehend the emotional upheaval they must have experienced as they encountered their mom with her deficits, limitations, and changes. What I had become accustomed to in many ways was a startling punch to the gut for them. I had done my best over the previous months to continuously keep them abreast of their mom's condition and circumstances but hearing it from me and seeing it in person was vastly different. Having established open communication as a family over the years, much to Judy's credit and her gift of talking, it created open opportunities to process, as they needed, what they saw, heard, and felt. Erika, Joel, and Seth were so thankful that their mom was alive and home but, at the same time, so much of their mom had been grievously altered. The distinct losses I had to face with Judy as my wife were exceedingly different from the distinct losses our kids had to face with Judy as their mom.

As their mom, Judy had been a pillar of strength. She had been mom with all the ginormous responsibilities that came with that role: home-school teacher, encourager, constant vocal support, spiritual example, and the glue, in many ways, that held our family together. Judy did not shy away from discipline when necessary but always communicated love in the process. Our kids knew, without a question of doubt, that they were loved by her.

Now their mom, who had embodied such a prominent fixture of stability, was fragile, disabled, unstable in more ways than one, and more vulnerable than ever. We expect our parents to grow older and for their bodies to weaken and change in the aging process. It's an unavoidable reality that we are forced to accept. At some point, the tides shift and we, as children, become the care givers and overseers of the very ones who spent so many years being the care givers and overseers of us. But for our kids, it wasn't supposed to happen this early with their mom. The tide wasn't supposed to turn so abruptly with such sweeping changes at this stage of life for both them and her. The wonder of our kids, though, is rather than shrinking back in grief, they leaned in with love and helped their mom feel even more at home because *they* were home.

Grandkids held an immense spot in Judy's heart. She had such "grandma" plans in store for the years to come. Distance wasn't going to deter her from being a very present and engaged grandma to our four grandchildren. With her life interrupted, her plans were put on hold but not her determination to still be present and engaged in the moment when the opportunity presented itself. That moment came with our kids' visit. Two grandchildren, Chloe and Tucker, made the trip as well. Knowing they were coming, Judy set her heart on one clear objective. She wanted them to sit on her lap and for her to read to them. What would have normally been a simple and sponta-neous activity was a monumental project for Judy.

One of the many deficits inflicted on Judy was that while her range of vision had somewhat improved post-stroke, she was often forgetful of or unable to locate the left margin on a piece of paper or a page in a book. The coordination between her mind and her eyesight didn't always collaborate with each other to find the new line to her left. Which, as you can imagine, made reading and making sense of what she was reading more difficult. Also, she experienced a strange stroke brain phenomenon where her mind pre-determined the words on the page and she'd recite those rather than the actual printed words the author intended. At times, this made for unintentional humorous plot adjustments in the story, but it was all due to the short circuitry in her brain. Not wanting that to happen when reading with her grandkids, she pre-selected 3 of her most favorite children's books that she loved to read to our kids and for a few weeks, practiced reading each one aloud. Judy practiced her audible cadence, her voice inflections and fluctuations, and slowing her reading pace to allow her brain, vision, and words to all stay in sync.

It was a beautiful success when both grandkids climbed into the recliner, nestled beside her, and she wonderfully read to them. The collaborative effort of me turning the pages for her and Judy intently focused on reading each word resulted in a heartwarming experience for all. Never had *We're Going on a Bear Hunt* been such an emotionally joyful journey.

* * *

The physical struggles that had plagued Judy in the hospital and rehab continued to plague her at home. No matter the deliberate attention given to her diet and my attempts to provide no or low-sodium foods, her sodium level would revolt against her. Familiarity with the symptoms would alert me to her condition, triggering an immediate response. While her sodium irregularities were not immediately serious, they required prompt attention as the situation could escalate quickly.

9-1-1 was my first go-to action step. Again, not because the situation necessarily called for an EMT response but because an EMT delivery assured us that Judy would be admitted to the ED (Emergency Department) within a reasonable amount of time compared to the indeterminable waiting as a walk-in. I dreaded calling 9-1-1. Even though I knew it was the best course of action for Judy, I hated pressing those numbers. Not because of anything connected with our experience with first responders but because pressing the "call" button put me outside the circle of control over Judy. She was no longer under my care, or my watch and I struggled letting go of her.

Predictably, every time a Medical Response Ambulance was needed it was either later in the evening or early in the morning. Never at noon when everyone in the neighborhood was unknowingly off to work. Instead, depending on the hour, they were all home or sleeping and so after making the call and receiving the dispatcher's instructions, I requested that the ambulance arrive with no lights and no sound. I didn't need the lights swirling and the siren blaring as they pulled up to our house. Upon arrival, I'd direct the EMT personnel with all their equipment and a gurney in tow to where Judy was anxiously waiting. As they walked into her room, Judy, being Judy, would graciously greet them as if they were arriving for a social visit. When asking her how she was feeling, she invariably responded, "I'm fine" which made me chuckle and I'd have to provide the explanation for her condition and why they were summoned.

Each ED trip resulted in, at least, a 3-5 day stay. It was never quick and easy, in and out. Arriving at and maintaining an acceptable sodium level took several days. Each UTI treatment was a days-long ordeal. For anything more serious than that, we were looking at anywhere from 7-10 days. By that spring, we were averaging an ED Hospital run every 5-6 weeks as we cycled through her physical maladies. Sadly, what was becoming apparent to me was that every hospital venture was taking a little more out Judy each time. After each stay, I was getting a little less of her back.

The ripples of Judy's hospital stays extended to follow up monthly appointments with her primary care physician, appointments with neuro and cardiac specialists, appointments for imaging, scans, regular blood and lab work, weekly home nursing visits, and normal checkups for a woman of her age. It seemed like we were in a lab, doctor's office, or being visited by nursing personnel every few days. All of whom, with good intentions, offered prognoses, opinions, and recommendations. The plethora of which left me feeling overwhelmed. I felt like I was losing my grip on reality and on deciphering what was true or most needed.

How reflective of that is life? The more we start giving our ear to the profusion of voices, recommendations, and opinions about ourselves from those outside us, the more we start losing ourselves. Our identity and the estimation of our value and worth become oddly shaped by the input allowed to filter into our soul by all those to whom we have given access. The result being we become a disfigured conglomeration of everyone else rather than the sole likeness of God who has made us to be us. Community input is needed and can be helpful for me to become a better version of myself but only as an additional resource, not my primary Source.

For Judy to move forward, I needed to remain as her voice, her information sieve. I was her unquestionable advocate but in being her voice, I needed to know what was true, what was most advantageous, and what was best. Her life depended on it.

Being Judy's voice, her advocate, her entire support system, and the other half of her left side neglect put me in situations that I would normally have never been a part of. As I previously mentioned, Judy needing scans and imaging was a routine part of our weeks. But that was far easier said than done. Due to the ongoing COVID restrictions and protocols in the medical world, imaging staff were not allowed to touch or assist a patient onto the imaging table. The patient had to do that themselves. So, try and picture me navigating a "stand/pivot"

Pirouette with Judy from her wheelchair and onto the horizontal table. I'm sure it resembled a contorted dance that was anything but graceful. My goal was to make sure, with every transfer, that Judy was safe and repositioned unhurt. Going from a sitting to a full horizontal position was certainly tricky but we accomplished it each time. Then, having to reverse the process was equally challenging and nerve racking as it all had to be completed under the watchful eye of our imaging technician. I'm sure she wasn't scoring me on my technique or Judy's perfect landing, but it felt like a performance awaiting approval from a judge. Before we left the room, my ego or self-esteem was hoping for a smile, a round of applause, or even a head nod from the technician to affirm the success of our error free routine.

Another such challenge that placed me in an out-of-body, other worldly context was the world of mammograms. Just saying the word, "mammogram" now triggers my anxiety. Simply because Judy had a stroke did not eliminate her from needing to undergo routine exams. So when the invitation for a mammogram appointment came, we went. Also, because a history of cancer ran in her family, it was necessary. My first exposure to that *pressure packed* situation, however, was not only startling but opened my eyes with a fresh appreciation of the complexities of life that women must endure. I thought a colonoscopy every ten years was rough.

For Judy, this exam was less than ideal or uncomplicated. For one thing, the examination room was barely larger than small walk-in closet. It clearly was not built with wheelchair access in mind. Getting Judy correctly positioned so that the exam room door would close and the mammography machine could record an accurate reading was intense. The machine was obviously built for a walk-in, not a roll-in. After being twisted, turned, pressed, pushed, and squeezed…me that is…I had Judy in place as good as she was going to be.

Maybe it was just me, but the A/C output wasn't keeping up with my amount of perspiration. Turning to the Screening Tech, I uncharacteristically blurted out, "Ready for take-off!" I never talk like that. After being twisted, turned, pressed, pushed, and squeezed…Judy that is…the exam was concluded, and we were released from our claustrophobic enclosure and on our way. I survived my first mammogram. Feeling flustered was an understatement.

Due to the amount of work it took to be out and about, we made the most of our time. Once in the car, we were free to be. Judy's primary request was that all her exams and appointments, as best as possible, be scheduled to end around lunchtime for the sole purpose of indulging in Chick-fil-A. That was one of her simple enjoyments. Those 6 chicken nuggets dipped in ranch sauce and a small Dr. Pepper were unbeatable in her mind. I believe, on a deeper level, they were hopeful reminders of better days to come.

Time was becoming an increasingly bi-polar presence. There was the internal insistence to slow down and make every moment count with intentionality and purpose. While in the same moment, there was the unrelenting pressure to be accomplishing more and that I wasn't doing enough for Judy's sake. Wanting to rest and just be with her was continually countered with the thought that resting was time wasted. Rehab therapy demands needed to be met, exercises needed to happen, and improvement and recovery success were an absolute necessity. Rehab missed was my fault. Exercises skipped were not acceptable. Lack of improvement was unsatisfactory. Time not spent repeating muscle movement activity with Judy was time lost.

The weight of responsibility was burdensome, and the fear of disappointment reared its ugly head. I couldn't comprehend being a disappointment and letting myself down and I couldn't bear to be a disappointment to Judy, but the truth was that being a disappointment was hanging around like an unwanted visitor who didn't know when to leave. The gravity of missing or failing my self-imposed expectations as a perfect caregiver and that Judy's recovery depended on me being so, was taking a toll on me. I realized it was becoming unhealthy for me and, therefore, unhealthy for her. I needed help. It wasn't Judy's fault, and it wasn't necessarily my fault. I believe it's the caregivers struggle but I needed a change of perspective. I was drowning, believing it was the only acceptable thing for me to do, but Judy would pay the price if I continued flailing underwater and gasping for breath.

Accepting my need for counseling was a healthy step in the right direction. I committed to weekly, 1-hour sessions. Walking into the counselor's office for that first appointment felt defeating as the false accusations started running through my mind.

"A stronger person wouldn't need counseling."

"If I was a better caregiver, I wouldn't be here."

"Judy deserves better."

"I'm a failure and a disappointment."

"I've messed up and now she's paying the price."

"I wish it had happened to me, not Judy."

"I've let everyone down."

My counselor immediately pierced through those bullshit lies. She didn't allow me to wallow in those false narratives of my life and situation. Instead, she proactively went on the attack to reframe my thinking from a failed underachiever to one who needed to let myself off the hook of perfection. I wasn't a victim of the circumstances, and neither was Judy. Through the course of those sessions, I came to accept, through tears and deep self-reflection, the fact that I couldn't do it all and that was ok.

It was ok.

Judy was ok.

I was ok.

I had put so much pressure on myself to do all the things, cover all the bases, be everything at once when, in reality, less was more. I was given permission to create space to slow down. That a missed morning of stretching exercises was not the end of the world. Missing our regimented pedaling therapy or bean bag toss was not going to make or break Judy's trajectory for recovery. And that missing those things did not translate into me being an ineffective caregiver.

Those powerful counseling sessions allowed me to see that I had been given no life training to be a caregiver. There were no pre-marital conversations on expected caregiver roles and responsibilities for later in marriage. There was very little pre-requisite experience that prepared me to even consider being a caregiver and so the expectations of being perfect were unattainable. I could let them go. Instead, I could shift my perspective to the reality that what I was doing in the moment was exactly what I was supposed to be doing. I wasn't behind or slacking, I was right on time. I was providing for and giving Judy exactly what she needed and was doing my best with what I knew at the moment and that was enough. I could let go of my performance-based expectations and all would still be good.

While my counselor was not faith-based in her approach nor used scriptural language in addressing my areas of need, she did, unintentionally, redirect me to my faith with God as my Provider and Sustainer. She pushed me to check in with my heart and soul. To do a much deeper dive into my core beliefs, or mindfulness as she put it, which brought me back to the unshakeable bedrock that I was not alone in my caregiving capacity, God was with me. Even though I was extremely weak, He was strong. Even though I felt so inept, He was more than "ept" to make up for any gaps. An aspect of that was being offered safety within the boundaries of my counselor's four walls to voice my fears, hurts, and frustrations with as much intensity as I needed and that God was not going to run away. He was walking through the valley of the shadow of death with all its rawness with me. With us.

* * *

Of all the pages written to this point, I approach these upcoming with the most personal hesitancy. Not because of any medical emergencies, therapy setbacks, dramatic disruptions, or abrupt interruptions to our lives but because of how intimate the following words are to my heart. I somehow feel that my words will not adequately describe or reflect the magnitude of what I'm attempting to say. I want them to capture the delicate wonder so clearly.

The stroke that impacted Judy's brain changed her. It robbed her of so much vibrancy and engagement with life and others. It reduced the functional capacity of her physical body to a fraction of what it had been. But out of the rubble, a new, priceless gem was unearthed which I safeguarded as a precious treasure to protect and hold so dear.

The alterations in Judy's brain clearly limited her ability to carry on conversations. Being one who never shied away from deep topics of discussion, she would eagerly dive in and share her viewpoint or beliefs on theology, current events and trends, faith, and life. She had a gift for de-escalating arguments and tension with her wisdom and personal life experiences. Judy could get to the heart of an issue in a person's life with compassion and empathy like no other individual I know. But that conversational ability to dialogue deeply was lost. She could no longer communicate at that level. Instead, there emerged an elementary simplicity to her conversational ability.

Please hear me, I don't use the words "elementary simplicity" as insulting or demeaning in any way. But rather, while Judy could no longer converse on larger, more substantial topics, her conversation became even more heartfelt. More sincere. More innocent. The small things took center stage and did not go unrecognized. She noticed the birds outside her window and commented on their presence and fluttering movements. The sound of raindrops from a rare California shower splashing onto a puddle was worth a moment of verbal reflection. The simple enjoyments of the view from a car ride or her deep, childlike abiding love for Jesus were conversational opportunities that she reveled in. Many times, her simple observations or genuinely loving statements brought me to tears. While I lost the deep Judy that I had become so accustomed to, I was given a gift to still be able to hear her voice express her heart's delights.

In a second area, intimacy lost was intimacy gained. Judy's deficits made physical intimacy an impossibility. That loving oneness was no longer an opportunity for us to express. Also, the stroke affects on the left side of her face inhibited her from puckering her lips to form a kiss. That didn't stop us from attempting to exercise those muscles, however. Her left arm neglect also prevented her from giving the type of hugs that she had previously so readily offered.

From the day I met her, Judy had been a hugger. A hug was synonymous with who she was. Coming from a family whose emotional reservedness was only matched by our reservedness over physical expression, Judy broke the barrier for the Foust family. She made it her expressed goal to give a hug to my parents with every visit, no matter how emotional it made my mom. Judy even, miraculously, was able to break through my reservations of personal space and instill the habit of hugging in me. If Judy loved you, you received a hug.

The loss of physical intimacy, though, was a loss that she and I both grieved over. But from the ashes of that loss came an unforeseen soulful intimacy that wasn't necessarily marked by touch but more deeply from the heart. It had been routinely customary for Judy and me to say, "I love you" and sincerely mean it. But never before had I experienced the depth and fullness of those words as when they were expressed by her during those post-stroke months. Her words touched my heart differently. They conveyed such vulnerability, tenderness, and unconditional acceptance. My response, in return, carried the inexpressible truth that she was my cherished world. The words, "I love you" wore much closer to our soul.

Intimacy lost was intimacy replaced with the hold of her hand as we sat next to each other enjoying our evening Netflix fix. Intimacy lost was intimacy gained every time we looked into each other's eyes. It wasn't youthful infatuation or a casual glance or even a look that spoke to 37 years of marriage. Judy looking into my eyes carried the sparkle of her life and reached my soul, communicating oneness, hope, and the fullest expression of who Judy was to me.

Strangely enough, I feel those months were the most precious, most intimate we shared together. I've told people often that I would have done anything to change the physical circumstances for Judy, but I wouldn't do anything to change that year of deepest, intimate connection between us. It was the sweetest season ever.

Every moment carried significance and importance. We continued to cling to hope for recovery and rarely talked about death's possibility. We weren't avoiding the reality of the subject but, instead, we were attempting to wring every ounce of togetherness that we could from the present day.

* * *

November 2022 marked a critical turning point. Over the course of the previous months, I had seen signs of decline but did not give up hoping for a miraculous shift in direction. As I already mentioned, each hospital stay took a little more out of Judy, making her more susceptible to infections and other concerns. She was simply weaker. Her body was declining.

Even though we adamantly and regularly started every morning with leg exercises to keep the muscles active and the blood flowing, Judy developed edema in her lower legs. It was almost unavoidable given Judy's sedentary life even with our persistent exercise work. To help combat her edema, Judy sat with her legs elevated and started wearing leg compression boots a few hours each day that provided massage and heat to help relieve the swelling and pain.

I noticed that it was becoming more difficult for Judy to take her medications. The muscles controlling and coordinating her swallowing appeared to not be as strong as before, making pill taking trickier. Previously pills went right down but now it was a struggle for her to move them to the back of her throat and to swallow. So, I had to resort back to crushing her medications to administer them to her. This was a noticeable setback for Judy.

On November 2, 2022, Judy was, again, showing all the familiar symptoms, (fever, face flushed, and hand tremors) of a UTI or sodium upheaval. And, again, late evening was approaching when the decision was made to call 9-1-1. Had there been a sign to indicate, the ED would have notified all guests seeking a room at the inn, "No Vacancy" when the ambulance arrived. With zero rooms available inside, Judy was initially checked in the ambulance and then moved to an ED hallway where she remained for a few hours. Given that she was, in essence, not officially a hospital resident, I was unable to visit her. So, I waited. Checked on her status. And waited some more.

Having finally had a room become open around 10pm, I was reunited with Judy and tests and procedures began to take place. With Judy's track record, the ED Dr initially thought her condition was due to a recurring UTI but that came back negative. Check.

So, the next best assumption was a sodium imbalance. But that came back negative as well. Surprisingly, her sodium numbers were in the safe range. Check two.

The Dr. then made the decision to take a chest x-ray as a precautionary measure to rule out any other possibilities. While precautionary, the chest x-ray, however, revealed a small abnormality in the left lower lung region suggesting a potential pulmonary embolism. With a history of previous pulmonary embolisms and being a stroke patient with flaccid paralysis on her left side, it all precipitated admission to the hospital. So, at 3:00am she was transferred to a regular room for further evaluation and treatment.

More tests and pensively waiting for results filled our next couple of days. As each test returned with a negative conclusion, we breathed a sigh of relief, but a mystery still existed as Judy's white blood cell count remained elevated. With this not being our first rodeo, I understood the process of moving from the general to the more specific in eliminating potential causes and narrowing the scope of focus. Finally, it was determined, to our great surprise, that Judy had sepsis. Having been informed of the seriousness of sepsis for someone in Judy's compromised condition, she immediately started on a regimen of strong antibiotics. That diagnosis confirmed that Judy's hospitalization would continue for several more days. Once again, that set off a domino effect…

Limited and interrupted sleep…

Muscle fatigue…

Trouble swallowing…

Failed swallow test…

Thickened liquid diet only…

Sedentary position…

Edema…

Skin wound….

We were repeating the same cycle all over again.

After 9 days and being assured that the antibiotic was aggressively and affectively attacking the sepsis, Judy was discharged with more medication and strict dietary and skin wound instructions. The mounting medical and care giver responsibilities assigned to me to cover and keep track of at home were increasing in scope and severity. While I was vigilant in monitoring her skin condition, I wasn't a wound specialist. I had, from the day she came home, been extra attentive to the heels of her feet, the coloring of her toes, any skin irritation on her back side or arms. Every morning, I applied soothing lotion over the parts of her body that would be in contact with furniture or fabric for extended periods of time to keep her body friction free. Every two hours her weight was shifted from one side to the other to reduce pressure wounds from developing. It wasn't going to happen on my watch, yet she came home with a pressure wound for me to treat. Needless to say, I became very familiar, very quickly with Medihoney dressing, gauze pads, wound ointments, and Neosporin.

Despite all my care giving diligence, our home stay was short lived. Just one week after being home, Judy complained of having intensely sharp pains around her left lung. The pain was excruciating enough that it prevented her from taking a deep breath without winching in discomfort. The only option I knew was a return visit to the ED and so we were back. Let me tell you, there's very little appreciative delight when the ED staff start recognizing you by name.

The go-around again resulted in another hospital stay for 6 days. More tests, blood drawn, lab work, and even a stress test came back inconclusive of any clear causes for Judy's discomfort. The previous sepsis was still showing signs of a residual presence and the stress test raised some slight concern for the cardiac team but not enough to warrant any further action at the time. So, 6 days after admittance, Judy was discharged again.

If you're keeping score, in the month of November alone, Judy spent 15 days in the hospital. It was all taking its toll.

Judy was tired. It had been 14 months of trauma, struggle, therapy, progression, regression, hope, disappointment, regained hope, hospitals, labs, scans, tests, blood draw scars, rough nights, better days, discouragement, and hope regained again. That last bout with sepsis withdrew more from her than she could counter. Her strength to continue the fight forward was overdrawn.

PART V

Fully Home

We made the most of the Christmas holiday by engaging in all of our favorite family traditions. Judy was resolute in making sure that Christmas Eve ended with Christmas carols and going to bed by candlelight. Her wish was my command. She was as excited as I'd seen her in years to open her gifts Christmas morning. She had the enthusiasm of a child. And she partook in our Christmas dinner as best as she was able. She fought with such admirable determination to stay up for as long as she could to keep that Christmas day in the present. It was as if she wanted to squeeze every last ounce from that Christmas in case it was her last. For her last request before bed, she said that she wanted to write me a note. So, finding a piece of lined paper and a pen, she scribbled these exact words…

"I Love you Eric Foust
    Judy
        Judy Foust
    Thank you such a goodChristmas Dinner!"

That note has become my most cherished gift.

* * *

The routine of January 21, 2023, began with giving Judy her bed bath, followed by washing her hair which she always enjoyed. She loved having her head rubbed with a warm washcloth and feeling clean. But this morning she seemed not herself. She was more lethargic and less engaged than normal.

Having transferred Judy to her wheelchair, she was having trouble holding her head upright and was visibly disoriented. To test her cognitive abilities, I began asking her simple questions that she would normally easily answer. But this morning, the answers weren't coming. Not only wasn't she answering the questions, but she, also, wasn't responding to any instructions. It was as if she was in a trance. There was no apparent connection to her external world.

My assessment of her condition immediately prompted me to call for an ambulance once again. Upon arrival at Mercy Hospital, our "home away from home," Judy's blood pressure was recorded at 80/39, indicating that she was hypotensive with a possibility of shock. Also, her heart rate was extremely high, as well as her white blood cell count. All these test results triggered immediate admittance with serious concern.

After several more tests and hours of waiting, the doctor arrived and asked me to step outside Judy's room to offer his update. He confirmed that her sepsis had returned with a vengeance and that the previous antibiotic wasn't strong enough to eradicate it from Judy's system. But also, tests indicated that her kidneys and liver were showing signs of distress and that her Potassium was high, and her protein level was low.

But the most serious concerns were that she was showing signs of pulmonary vascular congestion and pericardial effusion. Asking for a breakdown into understandable terms, he said that Judy was showing symptoms, firstly, of enlarged blood vessels in her lungs which usually coincides with heart failure and, secondly, an extra buildup of fluid in the space around her heart. Both were potentially life-threatening.

The doctor's words hit with such excessive force that I felt the reverberation throughout my entire body. Even though Judy and I had walked through the valley of the shadow of death many times prior to this moment, this is the first time it struck me that the shadow had become probable. I wasn't ready to face that chapter of Judy's story yet.

Now late in the afternoon and with Judy being exhausted, she easily fell asleep and slept soundly for a couple of hours. I was grateful for her time to rest. Close to 6:30, her evening dinner arrived. Feeling like she had slept enough, I attempted to wake Judy up, but my attempts were met with no response. I began calling her name with louder and louder emphasis while tapping her checks to stir her from what I could only assume was deep slumber, but nothing was working. She wasn't waking up. Rather than using the nurse's station call button, I ran to the hallway and yelled for a nurse. The nurse in closest proximity ran to Judy's room and I rapidly exclaimed that Judy wasn't waking up. The nurse attempted to rouse Judy from sleep as well but…nothing.

Upon failure to awaken her, the nurse pressed the hospital intercom button and forcefully announced the most frightening words I had ever heard, "Emergency, Code Blue. Room 245A. All medical staff, emergency, Code Blue, Room 245A!" Within seconds, medical personnel of all specialties were running down the hallway to Judy's room. The room immediately filled to overflowing. Instructions were given to clear out Judy's roommate to create space and seconds later, her roommate was no longer present. I have no idea where she was taken but she was out of sight. As organized chaos seemed to increase, a nurse gently grabbed me by the arm and escorted me out of the room. I'm pretty sure I was in my own state of shock.

Getting my attention, the nurse calmly informed me that it

would be better if I waited outside so as to give the medical response team as much room as possible to work. Finding a wall to brace myself from falling, it seemed like everything in my immediate world was collapsing into a black hole. It was hard to breathe and equally hard to focus my vision. The space around me was a blur. I had no idea what to look at or where to get my bearings. As one doctor was met by an attending nurse in the doorway of Judy's room, I heard the words "cardiac arrest" and "stroke alert." My brain couldn't compute any context or sentence structure, only those words. I felt like a solitary island in a raging hurricane.

As much as I tried to stifle my emotions with my hand covering my mouth, the sobbing erupted uncontrollably. I was an outside observer to life-or-death hinging in real time. In that turmoil of uncertainty, the second half of Psalm 23: 4 came to my mind, "Even though I walk through the valley of the shadow of death, *I will fear no evil, for you are with me*" (Psalm 23:4 NIV). I was not alone.

The chaos seemed to be subsiding and a normal pace was returning to the medical staff when the primary doctor asked me to join him in the small waiting room a few doors down from Judy's where we could talk in private. As he closed the waiting room door, he proceeded to inform me that Judy had, indeed, suffered a form of cardiac arrest but that they had got her stabilized. Her blood pressure had dropped to 50/42 and so intravenous fluids were immediately started. While, at first, they suspected Judy had suffered another stroke, that was determined to be negative. At the moment, she was doing better, and I was invited to rejoin her.

Judy was drifting in and out as I spent the next couple of hours with her. While her facial color was not as pink as before, she appeared to have come through that massive ordeal relatively unscathed. I stayed by her bedside until around 10:00pm when the nurse suggested that I go home and get some sleep. She assured me that they would keep a close eye on Judy and should anything change, they would call me. So, I kissed Judy's cheek and left.

Sometime in the night, my phone startled me awake. Quickly retrieving it from the small table next to me, I answered with a half-awake, half-frightened voice. The nurse relayed the information that Judy had suffered a second cardiac episode. Her blood pressure had dropped below 50 and so she had been moved to the Pulmonary Cardiac Unit for more specialized care and monitoring. She was doing ok, and I would be able to see her in the morning. Returning to sleep, for me, was not going to happen after that. Getting up, I prepared myself for the unknowns of the day ahead and waited anxiously for the first chance to see my wife again.

Arriving as soon as visitors were allowed, I rushed to Judy's room. She was attempting to sleep but her breathing seemed labored. Her struggle clearly appeared to have intensified overnight. Around mid-morning, the doctor arrived and brought me up to speed. After Judy's early morning cardiac episode, x-ray images were taken which revealed a large amount of fluid had accumulated in the pericardial sac around the heart. That fluid was essentially compressing the heart and restricting it from functioning properly. In the simplest of terms, the pressure from the fluid wasn't allowing Judy's heart to pump enough blood to the rest of her body.

The doctor continued to explain that, given Judy's condition, a pericardiocentesis was scheduled for later that afternoon. Pericardiocentesis is a procedure using a needle and catheter to remove the fluid from the pericardium around the heart. As a part of the process, a pigtail catheter would be inserted rather than a chest tube for further fluid removal. Post-procedure, Judy would be transferred to ICU.

The profusion of medical information continued to ebb and flow like the tide. At low tide, the lack of information felt like a respite, an opportunity to regain my composure and simply be. At high tide, the force of the waves and the draw of the undertow was difficult to withstand. The volume of medical wordage felt like I was being sucked out into the vast ocean without a rescue. At various moments, the reality that this was Judy who was being discussed snatched my very breath and I had to intentionally inhale.

With Judy back in ICU, it was as if we had gone full circle. Our unimaginable journey had begun in ICU with uncertainty and fear sixteen months earlier and now we were in the same ICU confines again with another invasive round of uncertainty and fear. The difference for this go-around, however, was that Judy was more fragile, recovery far less optimistic, and time was not working in our favor. I tangibly sensed, as each day passed, that the clock was winding down on any positive prognosis.

Three days into Judy's ICU stay, the dominoes again began to topple. Fluid was continuing to be drained from her pericardium. But then fluid was also found building up in her lungs which needed to be drained. Samples of that particular fluid were sent in for culture tests. After fourteen months of blood draws, blood tests, and IV needles, there wasn't a useable or responsive vein in Judy's right arm for an IV, so a picc line was inserted to administer medications directly to the larger veins around her heart. Due to the extreme lack of physical movement, Edema was also creating its own havoc for Judy. The swelling in her legs required constant attention and repositioning.

The next domino to fall was failing her swallow test. It was almost inevitable given her lack of sleep, physical decline, and muscle inactivity. With the failure of the swallow test and not having had significant amounts of nutrients in her body for several days, it was determined that Judy needed to have a nasogastric tube inserted to boost her nutrition intake. The process would involve running a tube through her nose, down her throat and into her stomach. While not painful, it is extremely unpleasant. At this stage in Judy's journey, however, nothing was easy. The ICU personnel did their best to insert the tube and have it correctly positioned in Judy's stomach, but her reflexes rejected it. After three volatile attempts and three fails, they gave up. One staff member made the off-handed comment that because Judy was an invalid, her body was involuntarily rejecting the tube and that they would make one more attempt when she relaxed again.

Having caught the staff member's description of her as an invalid, Judy looked at me with her tired blue eyes and said through her raspy voice, "I don't want to be invalid." Gently correcting her sentence structure, I questioned, "You don't want to be an invalid?"

"No," Judy responded, "I don't want to be invalid."

Again, thinking she was misstating what she was saying, I leaned in closer to intently hear her words and asked her to repeat what she was saying one more time. And with as much strength as she could muster, Judy said, "I don't want to be invalid. I want my life to matter for Jesus." As if on cue, the spigot of tears began to flow from both of us.

Here I thought Judy was misusing the word when she was using it exactly as she intended. She wanted her life to count, to have an impact, for her life to make a difference. As she laid in her bed in the tenuous connection between the temporal and the eternal, her immediate concern was that the span of her days reflected the life of Christ in her with value. I reassured her that not only were her days valid but that *she* was valid and valued.

Hoping for a rebound, the number of strikes against her continued to mount over the following few days. Fluid retention repeatedly amassed around her heart, her speech weakened, there was a more noticeable droop on the left side of her face, and her body was retaining all fluids. Judy's liver and kidneys were also showing signs of distress and she was sleeping more than she was awake. The one bright spot was that with the help of sedation, the nasogastric tube was able to be inserted on the fourth and final attempt. She was finally able to receive adequate nutrition. In the face of everything else, this was considered a big win.

On January 29, 2023, the doctor asked to meet with me outside the range of Judy's hearing. So, I joined him and the nurse on duty in the hallway. She proceeded to inform me that Judy wasn't rebounding and that they recommended a shift in direction from ICU medical care to medical management. The words seemed like semantics to me. That shift in direction, however, meant that Judy would be moved from ICU to the regular medial unit. With my ongoing permission, they would continue draining the fluid around her heart and in her lungs solely for the sake of comfort. Then she said the words I had been expecting but dreaded to hear, "Our best assessment is that Judy's struggle is coming to an end. The steps we take now will not prolong her life. Her condition is irreversible."

IRREVERSIBLE. After months of pressing forward to the best of our ability, leaning into the recovery that we had so longingly desired, and pouring every ounce of energy and strength into future hope, her condition was now irreversible. It was as if I and our kids were suddenly thrust involuntarily into the darkest days. The cavernous reality of death surrounded us. This set off a series of decisions and actions that no one is prepared to encounter until it's required.

The next day, January 30, 2023, Judy's birthday, I met with the Palliative Care Director. It was the most difficult meeting to date. The director compassionately and empathetically expressed her condolences for meeting under such heart wrenching circumstances, inquired into how I was doing, and communicated the unpleasant steps that we, as a family, would soon undertake. The pendulum swing from Judy's suffering being over and my impending grief was in full motion. At several points in our conversation, I needed to stop and sob uncontrollably. Judy was dying.

With my body racing with anxiety, my face and eyes red

from the convulsion of the early onset of grief, and my mind swimming in disbelief, I arrived back in Judy's room only to be met with the doctor and nurse at Judy's bedside. The next decision needed to be addressed. Checking her cognitive ability and finding her responsive, the doctor asked the question, "Judy, should it become necessary as a life-saving option, do you want to be resuscitated?" Pausing for a moment, she turned her head and looked at me with such a weakened expression and said with a whispered voice, "No."

Her answer did not carry despair or resignation but love and living hope. Her "no" conveyed for her the faith-filled belief that a transition was coming by which death was only the doorway to something far greater. She was ready. Judy didn't fear death. The doctor then turned to me and confirmed that we had heard Judy's decision correctly and that I agreed. I did.

How surreal it was that on Judy's 63rd birthday, we were confirming her approaching death.

It fell to me, as only it should, to call our kids and convey to them the unbearable news about their mom. Gathering all on a group call, I brought them current on where we were at as this part of our family journey was drawing to a close. Erika and Tim, Joel, and Seth and Ashlynne all agreed that it was necessary for them to fly to Redding and be present with Judy on her final days. Victoria, Joel's wife, wasn't able to make the trip and so a special time was scheduled for her to call Judy and tenderly communicate what she needed to express to her mother-in-law.

After consultation with the doctor, primary care nurse, and the Palliative Care Director, it was decided that Judy would be moved to a private room to accommodate our family and our need for privacy. This final move also precipitated the decision that she would be transferred from medical care to comfort care. Comfort care meant that all procedures, tests, and life sustaining medical attention would stop. Judy had gone through enough and now it was done. Instead, she would be kept comfortable and pain free. Eventually, she would be administered a morphine drip to eliminate any discomfort and she would peacefully fall asleep.

I had encountered death's presence before with the loss of my parents and Judy's father. I had also officiated several funerals and been with grieving families over the years as a pastor. But this time, with Judy, it was so much more personal. Waiting and watching as death took a more prominent hold on her with each passing day was gut wrenchingly painful. I hate death.

Being in a private room and with Judy receiving comfort care, removed all restrictions on visiting hours for us. We could stay as long as we wanted and come and go as we needed. One by one, our kids arrived, and a bedside vigil was established. With Joel needing to travel the furthest and with the cross-country coordination of flights and layovers, he was the last to arrive. By now, Judy knew that her children were coming to be with her and so she anxiously asked where Joel was. We assured her that he was on his way and would be there shortly. A few hours would pass, and she would inquire again about Joel's whereabouts. Reassuring her again that he was close, Judy would breathe a sigh of relief. It was clearly evident that she was hanging on and fighting to remain coherent until Joel was present.

With our kids at Judy's bedside, I gave each of them time to spend with their mom alone. I wanted them to, individually, have the opportunity to say all that they needed to express to Judy and for her to have a moment to respond. Her speech was becoming more slurred and sluggish, making it more difficult for her to be understood. She was also only able to stay awake for about ten minutes at a time and so being communicative and alert were priceless moments. It was precious and heartbreaking to see each of them pull their chair close to Judy's face, lean in, and have one last mom and child conversation. Even though Judy was extremely weak, you could still see the unconditional love in her eyes as she looked at her children.

The next few days were consumed with waiting and watching. It's brutal and almost beyond human capacity to watch your loved one drift further away and for death to absorb more of the person you so dearly love and hate to lose. It's an unfair exchange.

Existing in the space between life and death, sitting in the unknown of when death would fully arrive meant that I stayed present with Judy around the clock. There was no way that I was going to miss the moment of Judy's passing. I couldn't comprehend that thought. So, I stayed. As the calendar callously turned the page into February, our vigil continued. On February 2, 2023, it was evident that Judy was slipping from us. She was asleep more than awake; her breathing rhythm was increasingly shallow and weak. Her speech was no longer understandable even though she tried. In agreement as a family, we informed the nurse that we were ready for them to increase the morphine drip for Judy's comfort. This decision meant that Judy would soon fall asleep. The sound of her voice would no longer be heard, and her beautiful blue eyes would no longer be seen.

Even though Judy was incommunicative, our kids desperately held onto every present moment with their mom, holding her hands, gently caressing her forehead, and running their hands over her hair. Seth joined me in staying through the night. I recall so many countless nights that Judy spent with each of them when they were young, holding their hands, caressing their foreheads, and running her hand over their hair to soothe them to sleep in the darkened hours of their restlessness. Now, they were returning the gift.

In the agony of waiting, we consoled ourselves with memories and stories of Judy and our escapades as a family. The laughter offset our grieving.

The increasing margin between breaths created a palpable tension. At several stretches between the rise and fall of her chest, we contemplated if that was the last, only to encounter another inhale. That lingering between the thin veil of life and death continued for two more days. All that appeared to remain was the body relinquishing the will to live. It is quite amazing how tenacious the body can be to keep fighting for life.

With the late afternoon hours segueing into the evening of February 3, we were given a beautiful, heaven-sent gift. Judy had not spoken or shown signs of responsiveness for almost two days. The morphine was doing its work. But out of her dulled senses, heaven broke through for Judy. To our amazement, her eyes opened, and she emphatically said with a strength in her voice that had been absent for weeks, "I see him!"

"Who? Who do you see?" I asked in stunned shock.

"I see HIM! I see Jesus!" Judy replied with absolute certainty in her response.

In those words, it was as if heaven invaded her room and the curtain between there and here, between the eternal and the temporal, between seeing in person and seeing by faith was pulled back and Judy was given front row access to the presence of God. Those were the last words that Judy spoke. But none could have been more sweeter or offered more comfort to the grieving or more expressed the fullness of a heart desiring her Savior. For someone who loved to talk as much as Judy did and did it well, there was not a better closing sentence for her to share.

As the hands of the clock methodically crossed over into a new day, Judy's breathing was weakening to where it was almost imperceptible. There were no visible signs of any discomfort. Her physical deficits, which had received such constant attention for the previous months, were still. Her expression was peaceful. I fought to stay awake but with the warmth of the room, the darkness of the early morning hour, and the semi-comfortableness of my recliner, I dozed off for moments at a time.

At 3:30am on February 4, I felt as if I had been gently awakened by a hand on my shoulder even though no one was present. Perceived imagination or a spiritual prodding, I was grateful. Fixing my eyes on Judy it was clear that the end was near. The space between each breath lingered longer as I counted the seconds in my head between the intervals. Standing alone beside her bed, I clutched her hand in mine, and whispered in her ear, "I love you. It's ok to go. I'll see you soon." I kissed her check. At 3:45am, Judy's fight was over. The love of my life was gone. Death arrived but it had no sting, no victory. Judy was now fully home.

PART VI

After Death

I remember the first time my eyes laid hold of Judy. She was walking in the college cafeteria with her friend, Peggy. She was wearing a yellow long-sleeved T-shirt with red and white stripes. Her hair was longer than what would become her normal shorter length, but it was feathered perfectly. Her dark rimmed glasses couldn't hide the exquisiteness of her eyes and her smile was radiating. She had my attention as she carried her food tray to her table. Now, as my eyes laid hold of Judy for the last time, she still had my attention. Normal aging and a heinous stroke had altered her youthful glow but she still captivated me. She was my Judy.

Time ceased to exist. I touched Judy's face, caressed her cheek, half anticipating her to breathe another breath. In the stilled silence, the tsunami of grief began to breach my heart. For Judy, the journey was over. For me, it had just begun. The absence of light in the room, literally (room lights) and figuratively (Judy), created an immediate symbolic void for me. I stood motionless, not knowing what to do but weep. Standing in that fixed posture, the Apostle Paul's words came to mind,

"For I am convinced that neither death nor life, neither angels nor demons, neither the present nor the future, nor any powers, neither height nor depth, nor anything else in all creation, will be able to separate us from the love of God that is in Christ Jesus our Lord" (Romans 8:38-39 NIV). Judy was already encountering the fullness of that love, even in the moment of my loss.

After several minutes, I presume, I stepped into the hallway and asked for a nurse. With a breaking voice, I told her that Judy had passed. She stepped into the room and procedurally checked for lung sounds and heart tones and confirmed what was true. She expressed her condolences and gave me permission to stay as long as I needed. Our youngest son, Seth, had asked to be notified when mom had passed so that he could visit her one last time. Within minutes Seth arrived and our grieving as a family commenced. Around 4:30am, Seth and I walked out of Judy's room. It felt wrong to leave but life was already, unsympathetically, calling us forward. Having given one last kiss on her cheek and having said one last, "I love you, Judy," I closed the door.

In the hours that followed, previous decisions were put into motion. A hospital social worker called to confirm where Judy's body would be taken and to offer myself and our family grief counseling options. I had forgotten but, not surprisingly, Judy was a registered organ donor and so a representative from the donor network called and proceeded to walk me through that process and how Judy would continue to bless others. The funeral home called and informed me that Judy's body had been transferred to their facility and scheduled a meeting with us within the next couple of days. All those interactions felt like an out-of-body experience. Words were being said but I had no certainty that I was communicating clearly or retaining pertinent information. To be safe, I answered all the calls on speaker so that my daughter, Erika, could serve as a secondary backup to the conversations. Over the course of the day, friends and family were notified. The most difficult call for me to make was to Judy's mom. How heartbreaking it was to tell her that her daughter was gone but we comforted each other with the belief that Heaven was now her home.

Judy had requested and we, as a family, agreed to not hold a funeral or memorial service in California. We would wait and hold a small memorial gathering later in Wisconsin with family. It was also agreed that her body would be cremated. Knowing that I would not be staying in California, there was no way that I was going to have Judy buried in a location that I would, more than likely, not return to. Even though my faith held to the belief that it was only her body that remained, and that Judy was present with the Lord, I couldn't fathom that distant separation. So, my own impending transition meant that Judy would stay with me until a later point in time when interment makes more sense.

I am no longer a husband. I am now a widower. A title I did not want but now must accept. It is an unchangeable adjustment. Everything has shifted. I am alone. Single. My daily partner in life is gone. Having been a couple for forty years, counting our dating days and married life, facing singleness is daunting. I vacillate between numbness and reality. Grief is a fickle companion. It presents itself whenever and wherever it wants, without warning. In the frozen food aisle at the grocery store, while watching TV, when checking the mail, at 2:00am, and again at 4:00am. Time and place are inconsequential to grief. My consolation is found in the fact that the deep valley of grief is truly evidence of a deep well of love that Judy and I shared. Without love, grief would not exist. While painful and, at times, incapacitating, grief magnifies the gift that Judy was to me.

Reflection, I've found, is grieving's close cousin. In the midst of grief, you cannot help but reflect. And the act of reflection carries the honest assessment of life. It spotlights the joyful and the regrettable with equal intensity. I regret the mistakes I made;

the choices I engaged in that inflicted undue pain on Judy. She didn't deserve it. I regret any moments of ever taking her for granted. I regret catapulting my priorities, even good ones, above her importance. But joy is experienced in that not a single regret was left uncommunicated with her. Months before we arrived at her life's end, when she was still alert and communicative, we revisited and talked through our mistakes, failures, and hurts. More mine than hers. Honesty and forgiveness, confession and grace were poured out. The reason for this intentionality was because I couldn't comprehend arriving at a future point in time and longing for a previous opportunity that was unavailable.

There is joy in the indelible presence that Judy continues to have in my life. I'm coming to terms with the truth that after experiencing such a deepfelt loss, one does not move on from grief. You move forward with it. The idea of "moving on" from grief conveys the connotation that Judy's essence, memory, and impact will dissipate into the background like fog dissipating on account of rising temperatures. Better days will come, for sure, but she shaped who I am. Judy had more to do with the person I have become than anyone else. The intertwining of her life with mine has created an ineradicable, inseparable mark on me and in me. So, she moves forward with me. The thread that connected us from "youngsters" in love to Heaven's gain in her death, still connects her to me. Not a day ends without me saying, "Good-night, Judy. I love you and miss you." She will continue to make me laugh and cry and I'm so ok with that.

Over the course of writing these pages, I've struggled with verb tenses. When I initially started putting my thoughts on paper, Judy was alive, and we were still hopeful of her recovery and so her story was written in the present tense. It was current and playing out in real time. But halfway through, Judy passed away and the verbs shifted to past tense. If one could get angry at a verb tense, it was me. I hated transitioning to what was instead of what is. The grammar gymnastics of switching back and forth is probably very evident throughout. It reflects, I'm certain, my own emotional and mental gymnastics from beginning to end.

But not to be lost in the writing, there is a future tense unfolding. I am filled with gratitude for Judy and our love story. And, as I said, I will carry her with me in this new chapter of life that is opened to me. But what casts my vision for what is to come, in all its uncertainty, is living hope. Judy embodied it. Now, it's my turn. Having moved to Montana shortly after Judy died, I am now surrounded by family and grandchildren. I have the privilege of honoring Judy's legacy while continuing to establish my own. A legacy of future-tense living life humbly, honestly, and authentically.

In this state of living hope, I would be remiss, however, to not acknowledge that what helps propel each step forward into this "future tense" life is found in Job 19. In the Biblical book of Job, Job loses everything that was life to him except his very life. The unexpected whirlwind that blew through his life left him desolate. Everything was gone. All the props that sustained him were blown away. And in Job 19, Job is at his lowest point. Despair and hopelessness have set up camp in his heart and mind. But in that place of loss, grief, and uncertainty, he makes this declaration,

> *"Oh, that my words could be recorded.*
> *Oh, that they could be inscribed on a monument,*
> *carved with an iron chisel and filled with lead,*
> *engraved forever in the rock" (Job 19:23-24*
> *NLT).*

Job wants what he is about to say permanently inscribed on an indestructible source so that he never forgets and that it never goes away. The determination of Job cannot be missed at this moment. Job knows that his feelings will shift like the sand and that today's confidence can become tomorrow's doubt. So, Job wants this eternal reminder:

"But as for me, I know that my Redeemer lives,
and he will stand upon the earth at last.
And after my body has decayed,
yet in my body I will see God!
I will see him for myself.
Yes, I will see him with my own eyes.
I am overwhelmed at the thought!" (Job 19:25-27)

As for me, in the turbulent waters of loss, change, and a complete life shift, I inscribe it on a figurative rock today, for tomorrow's uncertainty, that my Redeemer lives and one day I will see Him as Judy sees Him now. I longingly look forward to that reunion. But for this moment, my God will see me through.

Eight months have passed since Judy's homegoing to Heaven as I write these final words. I sit daily with a cup of coffee at my regular coffee shop. Leaving my apartment every morning used to be an escape from the newly undesirable realities of my solitariness, but it has now become my routine. This coffee shop is my haven. I've become thankful for the quiet morning hours to reflect with gratitude on my life with Judy. It has been therapeutic and cathartic for me to remember and write. At moments, I catch myself hearing her voice or expecting her to come around the corner. Even though it's only in my imagination, I know she's with me. The tears still appear without warning or reason, and I embrace them as a present reminder of the precious gifts Judy and her exuberant hope were for me. From my current vantage point, the horizon holds more life for me to live and I embrace that truth with as much enthusiasm as I am able. For while life holds love and loss, joy and grief, marriage and singleness, they can all be given back to God as worship for Him to make more of than we can imagine. Living hope abounds.

"I love you, Judy."

. . .

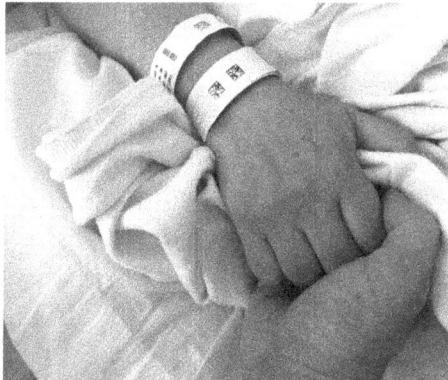

About the Author

Eric Foust was married to Judy for 38 hope-filled years. What a journey it was. He has three married children and four grandchildren. Having been a pastor, college professor, and an executive leader, Eric now resides in Great Falls, MT.